Publishing for Publicity

How to Promote
Your Business with a Book

ROY RASMUSSEN

and

MARIAN HARTSOUGH

PUBLICITY PRESS

Book design by Marian Hartsough
Cover design by Michael Tanamachi and Marian Hartsough

Disclaimer: This book is intended to provide information only, and should not be construed as professional business or financial advice. No income claims are stated or implied. How you put this information to use is up to you.

ISBN-10: 1-932311-57-2
ISBN-13: 978-1-932311-57-0

Printed in the United States of America

10 9 8 7 6 5 4 3 2 1

PUBLICITY PRESS
1285 Stratford Avenue, Suite G262
Dixon, California 95620
866-221-8408
http://www.publishingforpublicity.com

Contents

Part V: Prospect   129

Part VI: Service=Sales   143

How This Book Can Help You Get Publicity

". . .nothing has been so helpful in establishing my own career and generating a steady flow of business as the many books I have written on my specialties. . ."

—Bob Bly, "America's top copywriter"

If you're reading this book, you probably already know that your own book is one of the most powerful promotional tools your business can have.

- It's an instant attention-getter.
- It sums up what you can offer consumers that your competition can't.
- It establishes you as an expert, giving you instant credibility with consumers and the media.
- It collects your best testimonials in one place.
- It's a full-length sales pitch where you control the flow of the presentation and the reader is a captive audience.
- It's a headline, a speech, a seminar, a resume, a testimonial, a business card, a press kit, and a full-length commercial—all rolled up into one.

These are actually only a few benefits to publishing. In the first chapter, we'll explore no less than 28.

So publishing a book sounds great . . . but how do you do it? Unless you have a book proposal and an agent, it's almost impossible to get an audience with a major publisher. Even then, your odds of getting accepted are small, and your odds of your book getting widespread publicity are smaller. 10%-35% of books sold by major publishers get returned unsold, unread. 70% of books never earn back the publisher's advance to the author. The notion that publishing a book means automatic fame is fiction.

Fortunately, computer technology has created an alternative to traditional publishers that can generate publicity—not instantly, but effectively, over a period of six to twelve months. By combining digital publishing technology, the power of the Internet, and more conventional publicity strategies, it is possible for a small business owner to publish a book and use it to publicize themselves as an expert in their field within a year.

How does it work? In this book we're going to show you, step-by-step. We're an author-publisher team with a combined 50 years' experience in all phases of book production and promotion. In this book we'll teach you:

- How to pick a book topic that will attract your target market
- How to write your book quickly and produce it affordably
- How to promote your book cost-effectively without advertising through free publicity
- How to convert readers of your book into customers without hard sales tactics
- How to leverage your book for repeat customers, referrals, and escalating profits

Armed with this information, you can turn your expertise into a professional book presentation that will bring you a steady flow of media attention, customers, sales, and profits.

To put this plan into action, please read the entire book first so that you understand how the whole process of book production and promotion works. When you've got an overview of the big picture, start working on the details and moving forward one step at a time.

If you have any questions or require assistance, please feel free to contact us and we will be happy to answer questions or discuss how we can help you. Let us know what we can do for you.

To your book's success,

Roy Rasmussen, author, editor, and illustrator

Marian Hartsough, editor, book designer, publisher, and publicist

http://publishingforpublicity.com

PART I

Overview

Publishing for publicity is different than trying to publish a best-selling novel. When publishing a novel, book sales are an end in themselves. When publishing for publicity, book sales are a means to publicizing your expertise and your products and services, which may sell for many times the cost of a book.

This difference in goals entails a difference in strategy between traditional publishing and publishing for publicity. To arm you with a publishing strategy suited to publicity, the following overview will introduce you to:

- The 3 major methods of publishing and the pros and cons of each
- 28 ways publishing a book can enhance your marketing, promotion, sales, and management
- The 5-step REAPS method for publishing and promoting your book

Let's start our overview with a question it's logical to ask before writing anything: why write?

CHAPTER 1

Why Write?
28 Benefits of Book
Publishing for Your Business

When most people dream about publishing a book, they envision a *New York Times* bestseller and Hollywood screenplay adaptation earning them overnight riches. Of course the reality is that only a handful of books ever reach bestseller status. But even if your book isn't likely to be a bestseller, there are many compelling reasons why you should publish a book to promote your business. In this chapter we will explore no less than 28 benefits you can gain from publishing a book.

Direct Monetary Benefit from Book Sales

First let's cover the reason most people think of first:

1. Profit from book sales

To address this, let's try to get a realistic perspective on what you can expect to make from your book.

Traditional publishing

In traditional publishing, many people and forces involved in the publishing process get a cut of the profits before the author gets theirs. A percentage goes to the agent, the publisher, editors, indexers, proofreaders, book designers, printers, binders, publicists, distributors, and vendors, among others. Shipping and storing books costs additional money, and money must also be deducted when unsold books—often a third or more of the total print run—are shipped back and redistributed. The publisher's net receipt per sale is usually just over half the retail price of the book. The publisher pays the author out of what's left, at a rate typically around 6 percent to 15 percent of retail per sale.

So to paint a very rough portrait of the big picture, for every sale of a $20 book, the publisher may earn somewhere around $11, and the author may earn somewhere around $2. Given this, most publishers seek books with potential sales of 10,000 or more, and preferably 50,000 or 100,000. Agents and book proposals are used to screen out unprofitable books and discourage non-commercial authors.

You can use these figures to make a ballpark estimate of what you're likely to earn from your book if you go with a traditional publisher. If you're able to get a major publisher to accept your book, and you promote it aggressively, you may make somewhere between, say, $20,000 and $200,000. Which is okay, but it's hardly overnight wealth, and it's hard work over and above the work it takes to create your book.

Alternatives to traditional publishing

Computer technology has given authors two viable alternatives to traditional publishing:

1. Print-on-demand self-publishing
2. Ebooks

Both of these alternatives offer authors a greater percentage of profits. But they also entail additional responsibility, requiring the author to take more responsibility for market research, book design, printing, distribution, sales, and promotion.

Print-on-demand self-publishing

Print-on-demand self-publishing enables authors to take an electronic reproduction of their manuscript directly to a printing and bookbinding service. The printer can be contracted to print only as many copies as customers have actually ordered. This sidesteps the need for agents, publishers, and warehousing, cutting out several major costs of traditional publishing. An author may make in the range of, say, $7 to $15 profit per sale, as opposed to $2 per sale. If you can sell a few hundred or a few thousand copies of your book, that's not bad.

However, the author now becomes responsible for many tasks traditionally handled by a publisher, such as editing, proofreading, and book design. The author must also assume all responsibility for book promotion without support from a publisher. So when all is said and done, self-publishing may end up costing considerably for these services—up to $50,000 in some cases. And unfortunately some self-publishing houses that offer these services do not have professional quality control—to put it delicately—so you may be throwing all that money away if you pick the wrong company to work with.

So yes, you can make some money from self-publishing if you have a solid book and a sound promotional strategy. And you can also lose a lot of money if you don't know what you're doing.

Ebooks

Ebooks are even cheaper to produce than print-on-demand books, since there are no physical production costs. The only costs are those associated with digital production and services, such as software, website domain purchasing, web hosting, autoresponder services, and online merchant services. These costs are considerably lower than traditional or print-on-demand publishing, and the author may make 90 percent to 95 percent profit from each sale. At $20 to $30 or more per sale, that's a decent profit.

But the catch here is that you need to know how to produce a digital copy of your book and promote your book online. You will need to know how to use a word processing program to create the text of your book. If you want to add graphics, you will need to know how to import them into a text document or combine them with text in a digital publishing program. You will need to know how to export your digital manuscript to a format that can be distributed online. You will need to know how to set up a website, how to promote your website, how to process orders from your website, and how to handle customer service issues online. In short, it takes a great deal of technical knowledge to sell ebooks. And if you don't have this technical knowledge, you will need to hire somebody to perform these tasks for you.

The bottom line

The bottom line is, yes, you can make some money from sales of your book itself, but no, it's not likely to make you rich, and it certainly won't make you rich overnight without a brilliant book and a lot of hard sales work.

So why write a book?

So why write a book? If the only reason for writing a book was to make money from book sales, in many cases you would be justified in deciding that writing a book isn't worth your while. But when you factor in the value your book has above and beyond profits from book sales, you will find that while the direct monetary benefit of book sales may be small, the indirect monetary benefits can be huge.

Indirect Monetary Benefits

The real financial benefit of publishing is the indirect leverage a book can exert on your marketing, sales, promotion, and management. Through its effect on each of these areas, a book can function as a profit multiplier for your business.

Sales Benefits

Publishing a book lends huge advantages to your sales campaign. These include:

- Establishing your authority in the eyes of your target market
- Making you a household name in your field
- Streamlining your sales process
- Creating upsell opportunities

2. Expert authority and credibility

Creating credibility is crucial to any effective sales message. Identifying yourself as the author of a book on your subject gives you instant authority that provides powerful support to your sales pitch.

To illustrate, let's compare the perceived authority of two imaginary experts who are virtually equal in every way except that one has published a book and one hasn't.

Two experts are invited to appear on *Oprah* to discuss depression among college students. Expert A is a psychologist who has worked for 30 years as a student counselor at a major university and has enormous theoretical knowledge as well as extensive practical experience. Expert B has similar work experience but has published a book on how to counsel students, which she promotes through articles, interviews, speeches, seminars, and a website. Oprah introduces Expert A as an experienced student counselor, and Expert B as the author of *The 7 Habits of Depressed College Students*, which presents a 7-step program for curing college depression.

Which expert is going to be perceived as a greater authority by the audience?

Which expert is Oprah going to ask more questions?

Which expert is more likely to get contacted by publicists and prospects who saw the show?

3. Household name recognition

Advertisers know that when customers recognize your product, they're more likely to buy from you than a competitor. This is one reason we see so much money spent on silly ads that don't sell anything directly, but instill recognition through repetition of slogans and jingles.

Being an author brings that type of "household name" recognition. Even people who haven't actually read your book may become familiar with your name by browsing books in your category on Amazon or in their local library. When these people are looking for information on your topic, they will think of you.

People who actively follow your field will see reviews of your book, seek out your book, and follow up with reviews and inquiries.

And people who have read your book will remember your name and keep an eye out for your next book and your other activities.

4. Time-saving sales literature

Direct-mail advertisers have discovered that long ads can often be more effective than short ads because they give you more time to persuade the reader. However, even a long direct-mail piece is usually less than a dozen pages. A book can give you 200 or more pages to get your reader's attention, explain your benefits, overcome objections, and persuade your audience to take action.

Because of this, your book can become a time-saving piece of sales literature. Instead of spending an hour trying to convince someone they need your product or service, you may find it more efficient and effective to let your book do your talking for you. There may be other occasions when you don't have the opportunity or time to make a sales pitch, but you can still hand out a copy of your book. At events such as seminars, you can have copies of your book on-hand, ready to answer questions from prospective customers. And you can send out copies of your book through the mail and the Internet to prospects who have expressed an interest in your product or service.

5. Prospect inquiries from readers

One author who published a book in the mid-1980s was surprised that years and decades later, readers with questions were still calling the phone number listed in the book. Once your book is in print, it will continue to attract prospects and make sales for you for years and years.

Prospects who approach you after reading your book are especially inclined to buy from you because they already know what you're selling. If your book impressed them enough to make them seek you out, you have a much better chance of making a sale to them than if you were making a cold call.

6. Less cold calls

When readers come to you, you have to make less cold calls. If enough readers come to you, you won't have to make any cold calls. This takes enormous sales anxiety out of your life.

7. Higher demand

A published author is in higher demand than an unknown expert. When people see your name on a book, they will assume that you know more than other experts, and they will prefer to contact you.

8. Higher price

Higher demand means you can command a higher price. And you won't have to justify it: readers will come to you expecting it, because you're a published author.

9. Upsell opportunities

Even if you gave your book away free, you could still make a profit from it. How? Through upsell opportunities.

A book may normally sell for somewhere in the range of $10 to $30. However, your book may interest readers in other higher-priced products and services you have to sell. Audio and video products may sell in the $49 to $97 range or more. Speeches, seminars, and coaching and consulting services may sell for hundreds or thousands of dollars.

One graphic designer uses a book to promote logo design services that sell for up to $10,000. If you give away a book that cost you $3 to print and it returns you repeat customers paying $10,000 a sale, that's a hefty profit on your investment.

10. Back-of-the-room sales opportunities

Your book can bring in extra profits through back-of-the-room sales when you do speeches and seminars. In addition to sales of the book itself, placing a stack of your books on a table can encourage attendees to browse other products while they interact with you. Sitting at a table signing autographs of your book and answering questions is an easy way to boost your sales at speaking events, and to put your book in the hands of people in your target market who might read it and buy from you later.

Promotional Benefits

In addition to enhancing your sales effectiveness, a book can also increase your sales opportunities by conveying numerous promotional benefits. These include:

- Press release and book review publicity
- Requests for articles, interviews, speeches, and seminars
- Material for articles, interviews, speeches, and seminars

- Networking opportunities
- Demand for expert interviews and testimony as an expert witness

11. Press release and book review publicity

When your book goes into print, you have an opportunity to generate widespread free publicity through press releases and book reviews. Depending on your target market, your press release and reviews of your book may qualify for distribution through hundreds or even thousands of sources.

More important than the number of reviews you receive is their quality. If you send review copies of your book to other experts and reviewers in your field, you stand a good chance of getting free publicity to highly targeted prospects.

Book reviews can also publicize your book to two extremely important markets: libraries and universities. Getting your book distributed to libraries or adopted as a textbook can not only multiply your book sales, but also promote you to an ongoing, steady market of targeted prospects.

12. Opportunities to write articles

As you're writing the chapters of your book, each topic you cover represents a potential article to promote your book. You can release material before your book is published to create a pre-publication buzz, and you can follow up with additional articles to promote your book after publication.

As your writing gains circulation, you may also get asked to write articles by publications and websites specializing in your field. This is a great way to network and to bring your message to your target market, without spending any money on advertising. You may even actually earn money from writing the articles.

13. Opportunities for interviews

Publicity for your books and articles will also generate opportunities for interviews. With today's technology, you can often do interviews without ever leaving your home, using the phone and the Internet. With these tools you can broadcast your voice through thousands of radio channels and podcast sites, and you can even do television interviews without having to visit a studio.

14. An interview tool

What will you talk about during your interview? The answer is right in your book.

You can use your book to rehearse for your interview. Use your chapter structure to organize a list of frequently asked questions and answers.

You can also use your book to help your interviewer rehearse. Most interviewers run on a tight schedule and have limited time to research, so they will appreciate it if you can help them prepare by giving them an advance copy of your book and a list of suggested interview questions.

15. Speaking and seminar opportunities

Just as publicity for your book will generate opportunities for interviews, it will also generate opportunities for speeches and seminars. What you say in your book can be communicated orally to audiences in your target market.

You can create your own speaking and seminar opportunities by booking events. You may also find yourself getting requests to speak and teach from organizations with an interest in your field, such as universities, corporations, and trade associations.

Speaking events don't necessarily have to be live, either. You can record a speech or seminar, upload it to the Internet, and offer it as a free sample or a paid product. Some "webinars" command thousands of dollars per attendee.

16. Speaking and seminar material

When you get speaking and seminar opportunities, your book can provide you with material to talk about during those events. You can use your book to organize your presentation, guide question-and-answer sessions, and pitch products that supplement your presentation—including your book itself.

17. Networking opportunities

During the course of writing articles, doing interviews, and speaking, you will encounter numerous networking opportunities. Meeting others in your field who are already in contact with your target market is one of the fastest ways you can get your message out. You can gain quick publicity by establishing joint venture relationships with strategically-placed partners. You can also gain benefits and income by promoting their products and services in return.

18. Demand for expert interviews

When you become known as an expert, media interviewers will seek you out when they need an expert quote on your topic. This gets your name in front of the audience, and it also exposes you to media scouts who may be looking for guests with your expertise.

19. Demand for testimony as an expert witness

Depending on your field, the reputation you gain from your book may also lead to demand for your testimony as an expert witness. Being called to testify as an expert witness earns you money and adds an item to your list of credentials. If it's a high-profile case, it can also win you free publicity. This can have a snowball effect, because once you get called as an expert witness for one case, the odds increase that you will get repeat requests.

Marketing Benefits

Although the sales and promotional benefits of publishing a book are probably more obvious, more subtle but equally significant are the marketing benefits. These include:

- Increasing your knowledge of your field
- Increasing your knowledge of your competition
- Clarifying your thoughts on your topic
- Honing your sales theme
- Positioning you against your competition
- Test marketing your product or service

20. Increasing your knowledge of your field

In college, doctoral candidates must research and master previous literature on their topic in order to become a recognized expert capable of contributing innovations to their field. Similarly, a big part of doing market research for a book is researching what other experts on your topic are already writing. Doing this research increases your own expertise. It refreshes your knowledge, fills in gaps, and puts you on the cutting edge of current thinking on your topic. As you consolidate, gain, and refine your knowledge, you will start generating new ideas to propel you to the head of your field, and beyond to the next stage of research and development.

21. Increasing your knowledge of your competition

Increasing your knowledge of your field will also increase your knowledge of your competition. You will discover what your competition is doing, as well as what they're not doing. This knowledge will arm you with the information you need to deliver customers new value that your competition does not offer.

22. Clarifying your thought on your topic

A paradox of education is that you can often learn best by teaching. The same is true of writing. Hearing your thoughts out loud, or seeing them on paper or a screen, lets you listen to yourself, forces you to organize your ideas, and pushes you to solve any problems you discover. This clarity of thought translates into clarity on paper, enabling you to focus your presentation in a way that your audience can digest.

23. Honing your sales theme

The process of clarifying your thought will also help clarify your sales theme, or what marketing jargon calls your Unique Selling Proposition (USP).

Your USP is your answer to the question, "Why should I buy from you?" It is what is distinct about your product or service that makes it worth your customer's money and more appealing than what your competition offers. Your USP can take the form of a better price, more value, a better product, better service, better selection, a better guarantee, or a more targeted orientation towards a particular type of customer.

Whatever your USP is, the process of clarifying your thought as you write your book can help you put it into words. For promotional purposes, you need to distill your USP into a slogan of 90 words or less, so that it fits the space and time frame of the media you'll be using to deliver your message. This sharpens your sales message into a precise verbal tool for persuasion.

24. Positioning you against your competition

Honing your USP both defines your own unique sales theme and positions how you stand in relation to your competition. You can communicate to your customers precisely what differentiates you from competing products and services and why they should buy from you instead of someone else. It also helps you identify any issues your customers might raise when comparing you to your competition so that you can be prepared to address these.

25. Test marketing

Your book can also serve as a test marketing tool. Your book and associated promotional articles and speeches can be used to air new ideas and get feedback from your target audience. As feedback comes in, you can use it to guide your research and development and edit future editions of your book and other products.

Management Benefits

Apart from a book's external benefits in promoting a business, a book can also bring internal benefits to management. These can include:

- Providing an employee training manual
- Providing a sales tool
- Providing a customer education tool

26. Providing an employee training manual

If your book details your company's business philosophy, products, or procedures, it can serve as a training manual for your staff. You can teach your company's beliefs and values. You can explain product features and benefits. You can walk through procedures and point out what to do and what to avoid.

27. Providing a sales training tool

Your book can also serve as a training tool for your sales personnel. By presenting your USP, highlighting your benefits, distinguishing yourself from your competition, establishing your expertise, and collecting testimonials, your book can provide sales personnel with the information they need to make an effective sales presentation.

28. Providing a customer education tool

In many fields, managing the workflow proves much easier if the customer is educated about the procedures involved. For instance, a mortgage loan officer will have less work to do if their customer already knows what paperwork to bring them and how to present it. Your book can provide this type of information, educating your customers and making it easier to work with them.

Evaluation: Benefits vs. Costs

Now that you've considered the potential benefits of writing a book to promote your business, you're in a position to weigh those benefits against the cost.

Writing a book is definitely a major investment. It is not only a monetary investment in whatever services you need to get the book printed, promoted, and distributed. It is just as significantly an investment in research, time, and mental and emotional energy. It takes planning, patience, persistence to bring a book from concept to completion and then to your customers.

Is it worth the investment? Only you can answer that for your own situation. Here are some questions to consider in pondering that question:

- Would honing my sales theme into a book help me communicate my sales message and distinguish myself from my competition more effectively than I am now?
- Would presenting myself as the author of a book help impress my expertise on potential customers and media contacts and improve the credibility of my sales pitch?

- Would having a "book business card" to pass out increase the persuasiveness of my sales pitch or save me time in communicating with prospects?
- Would promoting my book through press releases, reviews, articles, and speaking opportunities help me reach more prospective customers than I'm reaching now?
- Would a book enable me to promote other products or services, such as audio and video materials, speeches, seminars, or consulting?
- Am I willing to invest the money, time, and energy it takes to finish and promote my book?

If your answer to some or all of the above questions was "Yes," you owe it to yourself to seriously investigate the possibility of writing a book.

CHAPTER 2

The REAPS Method of Publishing for Publicity

So you know there are many benefits to publishing a book. But *how* do you get your book published? To help give you an overview of the big picture, the steps involved can be represented by the word **REAPS**:

Research your market

Express your message

Announce your book to the world

Prospect for customers

Service=Sales

Graphically, this process can be depicted this way:

Research -> Writing -> Promotion -> Prospecting -> Service = Sales

Let's explore each step of the publishing process in more detail.

Research Your Market

Market research is the first step in publishing your book. During this phase you answer questions about:

- Your audience. Who is your audience, and what do they need?

- Your competitors. Who are your competitors, what do they offer your audience to meet their needs, and what do they fail to deliver?
- Your own position in your market. How do you stand out from your competitors?
- Your product or service. How does what you offer meet your audience's needs better than what your competition offers?
- Your brand name and image. What words and images can communicate the unique benefits your product or service offers?

Collecting this information helps you decide what topic will make you and your book most appealing to your audience. Picking your topic is the beginning of the next stage of the process: writing your book.

Express Your Message

Expressing your message is the process of producing your book in written form. This process includes:

- Picking your topic
- Naming your title
- Outlining your contents
- Filling in your contents
- Editing
- Visual aid design
- Layout design
- Cover design
- Indexing and proofreading
- Printing and binding

The beginning of this process focuses on writing the manuscript of your book. The middle phase turns your manuscript into an edited manuscript that is ready for the printers. The last stage turns your manuscript into a printed, bound book that is ready for distribution to your readers.

Announce Your Book to the World

Once you have your book in hand, your next job is letting your readers know it's available. You can announce your book to the world through a number of channels. Channels which can generate quick publicity include:

- Word-of-mouth referrals and endorsements
- Internet publicity
- Articles, newsletters, press releases, and book reviews
- Digital information products, such as audios and videos
- Speeches
- Seminars and coaching
- Interviews

These methods of publicizing your book give you opportunities to get your book into the hands of prospective customers, which starts the next phase of the process: prospecting.

Prospect for Customers

Prospecting is the beginning of the sales process. But unlike a traditional "pushy salesman" model, a sales model centered around prospecting emphasizes building a relationship with your customer step-by-step. The steps to building a relationship with your customer include:

- Introducing yourself to your prospective customer
- Getting to know your prospect and listening to what they need
- Evaluating whether what you offer can meet their need

- Offering to meet their need
- Agreeing on a fair exchange for what you offer

Once you've reached an agreement, your prospect is now a customer! The next step is following through on your offer and delivering what you promised.

Service=Sales

Delivering what you promised is all about customer service. Good customer service is what turns:

- A single sale into a lifelong customer relationship
- A single purchase into ongoing purchases
- A happy customer into your best salesman for referring you to new customers

Customer service is also the difference between a happy customer who will bring you repeat business and referrals and an unhappy customer who will drive business away from you. So there is a double meaning to REAPS, alluding to the Biblical phrase, "A man reaps what he sows." Marketing experts have taken to calling this the Law of Reciprocity. It is a fact of life that also applies in business.

Applying this principle to book promotion underscores why it's so important that what you write delivers your readers real value. If you give away valuable information in your book, you will reap the reward of readers coming back to you for more.

This overview should give you a big picture of the steps involved in publishing for publicity. Now let's break the big steps down into little steps and get into the first phase of the process: market research.

PART II

Research Your Market

Market research is the planning stage of your book. It's designed to make sure that what you say will appeal to your audience. To maximize your book's appeal, during your market research you seek to answer questions about:

- Your audience. Who is your audience, and what do they need?
- Your competitors. Who are your competitors, what do they offer your audience to meet their needs, and what do they fail to deliver?
- Your own position in your market. How do you stand out from your competitors?
- Your product or service. How does what you offer meet your audience's needs better than what your competition offers?
- Your brand name and image. What words and images can communicate the unique benefits your product or service offers?

In the following chapters we'll go into greater detail on how to answer these questions and use them to generate a marketable topic for your book.

CHAPTER 3

Identify Your Audience and Their Needs

When you write a letter or email to somebody, you always know who you're writing to and why. But you'd be surprised how many people write a book without considering these questions. It's a big reason why 10%–35% of books get returned to the publisher unsold and unread. If you want your book to be read, before you write it, you should have clear answers to the questions:

- Who am I writing to?
- Why would they want to read what I write instead of doing something else with their time?

You can answer both questions at once if you realize that the reason people will read your book is that you're offering something they need. When you factor this in, you can answer both questions at once using this formula:

I am writing to people who need X.

But how do you find what X is? And where do you find people who need X?

Finding Your Audience

To answer these questions, it helps to bear in mind how you're going to be promoting your book later. The channels you'll be

29

using to promote your book will determine who will be reading it—who your prospects are. This in turn will determine what those prospects need.

We'll get into promotion more in later chapters, but for now let's consider it as it impacts marketing. Where are you going to find prospects who will want to read your book? There are various possible sources, including:

- Your existing and past customers
- Customers of your joint venture partners
- Customers of your competitors
- Readers of traditional and online publications and information products in your field, such as articles, newsletters, books, audios, and videos
- Attendees of your speeches, seminars, and training programs
- Listeners to your interviews
- Audiences exposed to your community relations activity
- Audiences exposed to your direct mail campaigns
- Audiences exposed to your traditional or online ads
- Internet users searching on a target keyword or visiting a target website
- Mobile phone users

Which of these prospect sources will be the primary target of your promotional campaign? Focus your market research on the type of source that best represents the audience you will be trying to reach later.

So if you're looking for more customers similar to your current customers, you might focus your market research on surveying your current customers.

But if you're planning to promote your book in a traditional or online publication, you should study that publication to understand your market.

If you're planning to promote your book at your seminars, you might survey your seminar attendees.

If you're planning to run a direct-mail or ad campaign, you should do some test mailings or ad testing.

If you're planning to promote yourself online, you might put up a blog and survey visitors.

These illustrate just a few of the ways you can identify your audience by identifying the promotional channels where you intend to contact them.

Finding What Your Audience Needs

Once you've found your audience, how do you find out what they need? The best way is to ask.

How you ask them depends again on how you intend to contact them. For instance:

- If they're existing customers, you might interview them personally or mail out surveys, ideally with some incentive to encourage their participation.

- If they're readers of publications, you can study these publications for clues, such as which article topics are most popular, which ads run most often, and what subjects occupy letters to the editor.

- If they're attendees of speaking events, you can ask for a show of hands or pass out surveys.

- If they're to be contacted through direct-mail or ads, you can use low-cost methods such as postcards and classified ads to test response.

- If they're online, blog surveys work well, and blog and forum comments and frequently asked questions are also informative.

However you contact your audience, you goal is to ask them what they need. A good way to do this is to present a list of up to ten potential book topics and ask them what they'd most like to see covered. If possible, when they answer, follow up by asking them why that topic is important to them and what they would hope to get out of a book about it.

Once you know what your audience needs, you're in a position to offer to meet that need. But first you should check out what your competition is already doing to meet that need.

CHAPTER 4

Study Your
Competitors

Your book's quest for your audience's attention will face competition from other experts who want to capture your readers through their own books and promotional tactics. The best way for you to meet this challenge is to study what your competitors are already offering so you can offer something better.

Identifying Your Competitors

First, you need to identify who your competitors are. If you can identify five of the top experts in your field, it will give you a good basis for analyzing your competition.

If you've been in business a while, you probably already have some idea who your competitors are. To gather additional information, you can use a number of methods, similar to the methods used to identify your audience:

- Survey your customers and ask them where else they've shopped for similar products and services.
- Study traditional and online publications to identify popular authors and advertisers in your field.
- Contact public speaking bureaus to find out which experts give speeches and seminars in your area of expertise.

- Research media outlets to find out which experts in your field are popular on the radio and TV interview circuits.
- Search target keywords to identify which experts in your industry are popular online.

Since you are writing a book, you will be competing with other authors, so it will be especially helpful if you can identify the top authors in your field. Amazon.com and Google Books are great tools for doing this. Try to identify five leading authors. Ideally you should read their books, but if you want to save time, focus on studying their covers, tables of contents, first chapters, and other key chapters, which are often available on Amazon or Google.

Analyzing Your Competitors

Once you've identified your top competitors, you can ask some key questions that will help you compete with them:

- What audiences do they address?
- What needs do they address?
- What needs do they fail to address?
- What topics do they all cover?
- What is unique about how each of them covers their topics?

Asking these questions will help you identify ways you can stand out from your competition, which is the next step. Later on these questions will also help you pick a topic for your book and decide what topics to cover and how to cover them.

CHAPTER 5

Distinguish
Your Niche

The questions you asked when you were analyzing your competition help you identify areas where you can stand out in your market. Marketing experts, borrowing a term from ecology, call these areas *niches*: places in a market where there is an opportunity to fill a need not sufficiently addressed by existing products or services.

There are a number of tactics you can use to distinguish niches where you can offer something different from what your competition offers:

- You can talk to an audience that they've overlooked.
- You can address a need they've failed to address.
- You can offer a better quality value, such as a better product, service, benefit, selection, bonus, or guarantee.
- You can offer the same value in more quantity by offering more of a given value or by packaging multiple values together.
- You can offer the same value at a lower price to appeal to discount shoppers.
- You can offer a higher value at a higher price to appeal to luxury shoppers.

Asking these types of questions can help you pinpoint areas where you can offer your market something your competition isn't. The next step is to figure out what you're going to offer to fill the niches you've identified.

CHAPTER 6

Identify Your
Offer's Benefits

Once you've identified an open niche, what can you offer to fill it that's different from what your competition offers? You can answer this question through a three-step process:

- Describe your product or service.
- Identify your benefits.
- Contrast your benefits with what your competition offers.

Let's walk through each step.

Describe Your Product or Service

First, describe the features of your product or service in detail. Here are some categories you can use to help you generate descriptions:

- Physical properties. If your product is physical, what kind of material is it made of? What does it feel like? What color is it? What does it sound like? How does it smell or taste? How heavy is it? How big is it? How much space does it take up? How much time or energy does it con-sume? (This last question can apply to both physical products and non-physical services that require some time or effort.) Can you depict your product or service's physical properties graphically?

- Structure. What are the major components or phases of your product or service? How do they fit together? Can you represent them with a diagram?

- Sequence. Can what you sell be defined as a process with a numbered series of steps? Can you represent your process as a flowchart?

- Function. What does your product or service do? What goals does it aim to accomplish? How does it achieve those goals? What kind of resources does it require to meet those goals? What impact does it have? Can you illustrate your product or service in action?

- Personal qualities. Does your product or service have any personal qualities? If you are providing a service, do you have a spokesperson? (A spokesperson can be a real person, like late pitchman Billy Mays of Orange Glo and Oxi-Clean fame; a character played by a live actor, like Stephanie Courtney in the Progressive.com commercials; or a cartoon voiced by an actor, like the Geico gecko.) Can you describe your employees helping customers? Can you describe happy customers? If you provide a product, is your product personified? (An example of a personified product is Mr. Clean.)

Identify Your Benefits

Next, review your list of features and identify how they provide practical benefits to your customers. Do they help your customers:

- Save energy or effort?
- Save space?
- Save time?
- Save money?
- Avoid pain, fear, frustration, confusion, uncertainty, a tough decision, or the loss of a loved one?

- Learn something?
- Make money?
- Achieve a personal goal?
- Relive a happy memory?
- Feel comfortable or satisfied?
- Feel entertained?
- Feel informed or intelligent?
- Feel confident?
- Feel rich?
- Feel popular or respected?
- Feel loved?

Contrast Your Benefits with What Your Competition Offers

Finally, after you've identified your own benefits, go back and compare them with your analysis of your competition. What do you offer that's the same, and what do you offer that's different? Drawing attention to what's different will help you stand out from your competition and attract an audience interested in what's unique to your offer.

CHAPTER 7

Name Your Unique Selling Proposition

When you've identified what makes what your offer distinct from your competition, the final step of the market research process is to express your unique offer in words and images you can use in your promotions. The most crucial part of this task is creating your Unique Selling Proposition. Other ways to distinguish you from your competition include naming your trademark and branding your image.

Stating Your Unique Selling Proposition

Chapter 1 introduced the concept of a Unique Selling Proposition (USP): your answer to the question, "Why should I buy from you?" Your USP is what is distinct about your product or service that makes it worth your customer's money and more appealing than what your competition offers. Your USP can take the form of a better price (Walmart), more value (the Whopper vs. the Big Mac), a better product (Mac vs. PC), better service (Southwest's bags fly free commercial), better selection (DIRECTV vs. DISH), a better guarantee (Domino's Pizza's 30-minute delivery), or a more targeted orientation towards a particular type of customer (Curves). The questions in the last chapter were designed to help you collect the information needed to verbalize your USP.

For promotional purposes, you should condense your USP into a slogan of 90 words or less. This length allows you to fit your USP into the space and time frame of the media you'll be using to deliver your message.

In order to fit your USP into 90 words, you should select keywords that capture its essential elements in as few words as possible. "Subway: Eat fresh." You can shorten phrases by building adjectives into more precise nouns and rewording passive prepositions as active verbs.

You can personalize your USP by building second-person phrases like "you" or "your" into it, addressing your audience directly. "You're in good hands with Allstate." Use commands to call your audience to action. "American Express: Don't leave home without it."

Make your USP memorable by using poetic devices. Create rhythm by repeating consonant sounds, rhyming vowels, and measuring meter. "Winston tastes good like a cigarette should." Wordplay, humor, and symbolism can add style. "Prudential: Get a piece of the rock." But beware of trying so hard to sound clever that you bury your sales message beneath a bad joke. "Capital One: What's in your wallet?"

Naming Your Trademark

You can support your USP with other methods of standing out from the competition. One effective method is to give your unique spin on your product or service a name that serves as a trademark. For instance Dr. Al Sears distinguished his method of interval training from competing exercise programs by naming it P.A.C.E. (Progressively Accelerating Cardiopulmonary Exertion).

Branding Your Image

Another way to support your USP is by branding yourself with a distinctive image. The image can be a picture (the Nike swoosh), a stylized letter or word (McDonald's Golden Arches), a character exemplifying some personality trait (the Brawny Man), a story (the story of Jared from Subway), or a combination of the above (Superman).

Building Your USP into Your Book

For the author, the purpose of doing all this market research and developing a USP is to build your USP into your book. Publishing a book provides you with powerful ways to convey your USP to your target market. Your book lets you communicate your USP through:

- Your title
- Your front cover image
- Your back cover blurb
- Your dust jacket
- Your table of contents
- Your chapter titles
- Your subtitles
- Your text
- Your visual aids
- Your promotional material

So armed with your USP as a solid foundation for your publicity campaign, let's move on to the next stage of the publishing process: writing your book.

PART III

Express Your Message

Your market research provided you with a Unique Selling Proposition to capture your audience's attention and outshine your competition. Now it's time to build your USP into your book so that your message permeates your pages from your title to your back cover.

Creating your book is a three-stage process:

1. Writing: Creating a manuscript. This stage begins with picking your book topic, takes you through naming your title and outlining your chapters, and culminates with expanding your outline into actual paragraphs and sentences.

2. Editing and design: Polishing your manuscript into a form that you can take to the printers. This stage includes editing your text, adding visual aids, laying out the look of your pages and cover, adding an index, and proofreading.

3. Printing and binding: The last stage is printing your proofread pages out and binding them together into a book with your name on the cover.

Let's break these stages down into smaller steps and see what's involved in each one.

CHAPTER 8

Pick Your Topic

During your market research, you collected information about what topics were in demand with your audience. You also researched how your competition was already addressing these topics. This, along with your USP, provides you with the information you need to pick your own winning book topic.

To pick a book topic that will effectively promote your business, you need to:

- Pick a topic in demand with your audience.
- Say something valuable about that topic your competition isn't saying.
- Emphasize information that promotes your USP.

To illustrate how this works, let's compare the seven top-selling diet books of 2009:

1. Jillian Michaels, *Master Your Metabolism: The 3 Diet Secrets to Naturally Balancing Your Hormones for a Hot and Healthy Body*
2. Liz Vaccariello, Cynthia Sass, and David L. Katz, M.D. M.P.H., *Flat Belly Diet!*
3. David Kessler, *The End of Overeating: Taking Control of the Insatiable American Appetite*
4. Alicia Silverstone and Neil D. Barnard, M.D., *The Kind Diet: A Simple Guide to Feeling Great, Losing Weight, and Saving the Planet*

5. Elisabeth Hasselbeck and Peter Green, *The G-Free Diet: A Gluten-Free Survival Guide*
6. Ian K. Smith, M.D., *The 4-Day Diet*
7. Paul McKenna, *I Can Make You Thin: The Revolutionary System Used by More Than 3 Million People*

All of these books focus on the same popular topic: dieting. Their titles are worded to appeal to the desires underlying the demand for dieting information. Michaels' subtitle appeals to two desires common to many of the other titles: to look attractive and to feel healthy. Silverstone adds an appeal to ecological concerns. Smith appeals to the desire to lose weight quickly.

Although all these books focus on the same general topic of dieting, each of these books emphasizes something unique not emphasized by the other books. Michaels emphasizes metabolism. Vaccariello emphasizes a flat belly. Kessler emphasizes appetite control.

These unique emphases promote their books' USPs. Michaels, leveraging her exercise reputation, is using her book to carve out a niche in the diet market by offering hormone balance as a weight-loss solution. Vaccariello is offering a solution for belly fat. Kessler is offering a solution for overeating.

You may have noticed that these books' titles immediately communicate their USPs. If you were in the market for a gluten-free diet and you saw all of the books above on a shelf, one title would instantly jump out at you from the others. This underscores how choosing the right title is crucial to attracting the interest of your target audience, bringing us to the topic of our next chapter.

CHAPTER 9

Name Your Title

You saw in the last chapter how a book title can instantly communicate the book's USP. In this chapter you'll learn how to design a marketable title that captures your USP.

Building Blocks of a Marketable Title

What makes a title marketable? In earlier chapters we talked about identifying your market, pinpointing a need in your market, and offering a unique solution to that need. A marketable title can contain any or all of these elements:

- Who your market is: For example, let's say your market is "high school girls." You could make that part of the title.
- What their need is: "High School Girls Who Suffer from Low Self-Confidence."
- How you're offering to meet that need with specific benefits: "Empowerment Tips for High School Girls Who Suffer from Low Self-Confidence."

You may also include other elements of your sales message, such as credential-builders like "proven" or risk-reducers like "guaranteed."

Building Your Main Title and Subtitle

Sometimes including all these elements in the title would make it too long or too bland. In this case you may choose to move some or all of these elements to a subtitle. For instance we could improve our title example by making it a subtitle and creating a more colorful main title:

> Girl Power!
> Empowerment Tips for High School Girls Who Suffer from Low Self-Confidence

We can likewise reword the subtitle. For instance, we might shift the focus from the need being addressed to the benefit being offered:

> Girl Power!
> How to Be the Most Confident Girl at Your High School

You can also use one or more subtitles to attract niche audiences who are not the focus of your main title. For instance, a book called "Small Business Success Secrets for Women" might address specific audiences by adding a subtitle, "Money-Making Tips for Single Girls, Stay-at-Home Moms, and Retired Widows."

Refining Your Wording

Once you have some idea what you want your title to emphasize, how do you choose your exact wording? There are a number of common methods. Here are a few formulas that are easy to use and work effectively:

- Ask a question about the problem your book offers to solve: "How Can I Overcome Public Speaking Anxiety?"
- Offer your solution as a numbered set of secrets, steps, or ways: "7 Steps to Public Speaking without Fear."

- Offer your solution as a numbered set of mistakes to avoid: "The 6 Greatest Fears of Public Speakers (and How to Avoid Them)."
- Offer your solution as a practical how-to guide: "How to Overcome Public Speaking Anxiety."

These are just a few ways to generate a title. Use these examples to inspire your own ideas. You can use these formulas as starters to create a working version of your title and then reword it to make it stronger if you want. "7 Steps to Public Speaking without Fear" could become "7 Steps to Speaking Fearlessly."

The title on your cover is the real beginning of your book. In the next chapter we'll turn the page and start writing the inside.

CHAPTER 10

Outline
Your Contents

From your title, let's move on to your table of contents. Creating a table of contents is creating an outline for your book. You can simplify the process of outlining your table of contents by using a five-step approach:

1. Choose a format for your book.

2. Map out the general structure of your contents as major parts of your book.

3. Break the parts down into a list of chapter topics.

4. Break each chapter down into subtopics.

5. Name your parts, chapters, and subchapter headings.

Choose a Format for Your Book

During the course of publishing history, a number of book formats have displayed enduring popularity and come to enjoy familiarity with a widespread audience. If your book topic naturally fits into one of these formats, you can study previously published books in that format for ideas on how to structure your book.

Common book formats fall into a few broad categories based on target market and distribution method:

- Trade books. A trade book is a book intended to be sold through commercial booksellers to the general public.
- Subscription-only books. These are typically reference works, such as encyclopedias. They are usually sold directly by the publisher to libraries and general consumers.
- Textbooks. These are sold by commercial publishers or university presses to students and libraries.
- Scholarly books. These are sold by university presses primarily to academic libraries for use by university professors and graduate students.
- Religious books. These include Bibles, other sacred texts, and songbooks. They may be distributed through commercial booksellers or through specialized channels servicing religious institutions and consumers.

Within these broad categories, particularly trade books, there is a wide variety of popular nonfiction formats:

- Reference books. This includes encyclopedias and computer user's guides.
- Science and nature books.
- How-to books. This is a huge category that includes numerous formats such as exercise instructions, consumer medical tips, relationship advice, parenting tips, cookbooks, home improvement guides, automotive manuals, language learning courses, home buying tips, investment advice, home business guides, and business leadership tips.
- Self-help books.
- Workbooks.

- Religious and inspirational books.
- Art books. These encompass all types of arts, including drawing, painting, photography, music, and performing arts.
- Recreational books, covering hobbies, games, and sports.
- Travel guides.
- Biographies.
- History books, including company histories.

Some of these formats lend themselves well to particular industries. For instance, the reference book format used in the *For Dummies* series has worked well for computer books.

Some formats might work well for showcasing your business. For instance, a restaurant owner might publish a cookbook sampling their best recipes. Or an illustrator might publish a portfolio displaying their best work.

If your book topic fits naturally into an established format, you can find samples of previously published books to study their tables of contents for outline ideas. You can cover much of the same general contents as previous authors if you can find somewhere to give a topic a distinctive twist.

Map Out the Parts of Your Book

There are many ways to begin an outline. Here are a few simple methods that work well for outlining books:

- List the major topics you want to cover as a path leading from a problem to a solution. For instance, a book on how to improve business management skills might start by discussing common problems faced by inexperienced managers.

- List your topics as a series of steps in a process. Example: Step 1: How to define your business management vision. Step 2: How to write a management plan. Step 3: How to manage your time. Etc.

- List your topics in order of learning difficulty. Example: 1: How to manage yourself. 2: How to manage one-on-one interviews. 3: How to manage group meetings.

- List your topics in the order you learned them. Example: 1: How I got started in management. 2: My biggest mistake in my early management career. 3: My first head management job.

- List a series of practical exercises related to your list of topics. Example: Exercise 1: How to manage your goals. Exercise 2: How to manage your calendar. Exercise 3: How to manage your email.

Some writers will find it easier to apply these methods by writing their outline down in words. Others will find it easier to draw them out as diagrams, flowcharts, or pictures. Others might find it easier to talk their thoughts out loud, to a recorder, or with another person. Others might find it helps to act out ideas as imaginary dialogues between their hands. Use whatever works for you.

These methods of starting your outline will produce the largest divisions of your book, usually called Part I, Part II, Part III, etc. Each part will then include chapters within it. Whether a division should be a part or a chapter will depend on how broad it is. For instance, in the above example of topics organized by order of difficulty, "How to manage yourself" is broad in scope and would probably be a part including multiple chapters covering various aspects of self-management, such as motivation, goal-setting, time management, etc. But the practical exercises for calendar management and email management could be viewed as related to the topic of time management, and might end up grouped together under that heading.

List Your Chapter Topics

Once you've created a general outline, you can start breaking down your material into chapters.

A chapter is ideally about 10 pages long, which fits the average reader's attention span. You may sometimes find it preferable to write a shorter chapter, as we often do in this book to avoid packing too much information into one chapter. But don't go too much longer or you risk overwhelming or boring the reader.

How-to books by major publishers average about 200 pages, or 20 chapters. Self-published books produced through print-on-demand publishers are most economical at just over 100 pages. 80-200 pages is the most practical range for print-on-demand books, though anything from 48 to 828 pages is theoretically possible. 80 pages is the minimum if you want to include text on the spine.

To expand your outline into chapters, take each part of your outline and start listing topics related to that part of your book. For instance, a book on real estate might have a part called "Learning the Law" with chapter listings such as:

- Chapter 1: Survey Says: How Land Is Described
- Chapter 2: A Man's Home Is His Castle—Or Is It? Interests and Estates
- Chapter 3: Nine-Tenths of the Law: Ownership
- Chapter 4: The Taxman Cometh: Taxes and Liens
- Chapter 5: Sign Here, Please: Contracts
- Chapter 6: Selling the Farm: Transfer of Title and Deeds
- Chapter 7: Licensed to Sell: Licensing Laws
- Chapter 8: See My Agent: Brokerage and Agency

Continue listing topics until you have covered the major points for each topic. When you're done:

- Review your list of topics to make sure you've covered all the main points.

- Add any missing points.
- Group related points together.
- Eliminate points that don't fit into your main theme and subthemes. You can save these for other books or articles, so you might still want to record them somewhere.

If you find yourself having too few topics to fill enough chapters, consider breaking some of your topics into smaller topics. If you find yourself having too many, consider grouping topics together or saving some for promotional articles or another book.

Your list of chapters should include an introduction and a conclusion, which are crucial to setting the overall tone of your book. Depending on your book, you may also include additional front matter and back matter, such as a foreword or appendices.

List Your Subtopics

A 10-page chapter will typically include about 15 major subtopics. A good rule of thumb is to start with a list of 18 to 20 subtopics and remove the least vital ones. If you can make three major points and fill up about two-thirds of a page for each subtopic, you can fill enough pages to finish a 10-page chapter. As with your page count, the number of pages and subtopics per chapter can vary with the unique needs of your book. The chapter you're reading now is only about eight typeset pages, but you'll probably agree that it's enough information for you to absorb at one time.

Once you have your list of subtopics, arrange them in the order that makes most sense.

So for example, a book on personal finance might have a chapter on investment with the subtopics:

- Investment goals
- Investment strategy

- Investment mix selection
- Cash and cash instruments
- Local real estate
- Non-local real estate
- Stocks
- Gold coins
- Gold shares
- Diamonds
- Bonds
- Annuities
- Collectibles
- Other opportunities
- Investments to avoid

We'll get into how you turn your subtopics into actual paragraphs and sentences in the next chapter. First there's one last thing to do with the parts of your outline: naming them.

Name Your Parts, Chapters, and Subchapter Headings

When you first jot down your parts, chapters, and subchapters, you should use whatever words you need to clearly state what topics you intend to cover. But when you edit your table of contents, you should remember that the table of contents is one of the first things a reader looks at after looking at your book's title and cover. Because of this, it's good marketing to name your chapter headings and subheadings using the same principles you used to name your title. Focus on your audience, their needs, and offering solutions to those needs.

However, don't feel compelled to come up with a fancy title for every chapter when it's not appropriate. It's usually more important to be clear than clever.

Once you've got your contents outlined, it's time to start filling your outline in with actual content.

CHAPTER 11

Fill in Your Contents

Filling your outline in with content is simply a matter of expanding your subtopics into paragraphs and sentences. This chapter will suggest some tips on how to do that, and what to do when you run up against writer's block.

How to Fill in Your Outline

The last chapter suggested outlining about 15 subtopics per chapter. As mentioned, this was a rule of thumb, adaptable to the needs of your book. However many subtopics you outlined, here is a three-step process you can use to turn each subtopic into paragraphs and sentences:

1. For each subtopic, write down a statement.
2. Restate each statement as a question.
3. Write down three points in answer to each question.

So for example, we could take the subtopic, "using a mouse," and make the statement, "There are several ways to use a mouse." That statement can be rephrased as a question, "How many ways can you use a mouse?" That question might generate the answers, "left-click," "right-click," and "scroll wheel."

Now in point of fact, there are more than three ways to use a mouse. As this illustrates, sometimes you can come up with more than three points in answer to a question. The purpose of trying to come up with three points is to help you write, not to limit you. Use this formula if it helps you, but don't feel bound by it.

If you apply this method one chapter at a time, one page at a time, your book will emerge faster than you think. When you have a clear outline of what you want to say in mind, the physical act of typing a page of 250 to 400 words can take 5 to 15 minutes or less depending on your typing speed. Even a slow typist is physically capable of typing a 10-page chapter a day provided they know what they want to say. If you persevere sentence by sentence, paragraph by paragraph, page by page, your pages will soon grow into chapters, and your chapters will come together into a book with your name on the cover.

Paragraph Structure

Each paragraph should express one major idea. You can express the idea through a number of formats, including:

- Questions and answers
- A series of statements
- Discussion of an example
- Commentary on a quote, anecdote, or story
- A bulleted or numbered list
- A quiz
- An exercise
- A checklist

The reader's eye is naturally drawn towards the beginning of your paragraph, so it's a good idea to put your main idea there. If you use this format, the following sentences can expand on your main idea.

However, sometimes you may choose to delay the introduction of your main idea until later in your paragraph. For instance, you might want to introduce an illustration before stating the point you're trying to illustrate. Or you might want to build towards a dramatic conclusion and save the punch line for the end.

Use transitional phrases to tie your paragraphs together and make them flow. Transitions include phrases that:

- Build on your previous paragraph: "and," "also," "plus," etc.
- Contrast with your previous paragraph: "but," "however," "despite this," etc.
- Change direction from your previous paragraph: "on another note," "elsewhere," "meanwhile," etc.

Transitions keep your paragraphs flowing so that the reader keeps reading and following your train of thought. Transitions can also help forge links between the individual sentences in your paragraph.

Sentence Style

Good sentences say what they mean directly and clearly. Use simple grammar and everyday vocabulary to get your point across efficiently.

Here are some guidelines to help improve your sentence style:

- Write as if you were talking to someone out loud. Using "I," "we," and "you" can help get you in the right frame of mind.
- Rely primarily on nouns and verbs and simple noun-verb structures, as in the sentence, "The fox jumped." Avoid unnecessary passive structures and prepositional phrases, like "The dog was jumped over by the fox."
- Select precise nouns. Minimize use of adjectives by building their meaning into your nouns. Say "the fox" instead of "the bushy-tailed, sharp-snouted dog-like mammal."

- Use active verbs when possible. Avoid passive verbs except when appropriate for grammar, emphasis, or rhythm. Passive verbs are sometimes appropriate under these exceptional circumstances, but normally they should be sparse. Say "the fox jumped over the dog" instead of "the dog was jumped over by the fox."

- Select precise verbs. Minimize use of adverbs by building precision into your verbs. Say "leaped" instead of "jumped suddenly upward from the ground."

- Avoid long words when short ones will do. Say "foxy" instead of "vulpecular."

- Eliminate extra words when you can say the same thing in less space. Say "The quick brown fox jumped over the lazy dog" instead of "The reclining canine, yawning lethargically, was aerially transversed by the speedily-moving earth-colored representative of the rival tribe of the Canidae family."

- Use everyday language instead of jargon. Say "fox" instead of "canid" or *Vulpes fulva*.

- Avoid overused figures of speech. Say "cunning" instead of "crazy like a fox."

For more tips, consult Strunk and White's *The Elements of Style*.

How to Break through Writer's Block

As you start fleshing out your chapter outline with actual paragraphs and sentences, you will sometimes get stuck wondering what to say. This is called "writer's block" and it happens to all writers, even bestselling authors. Fortunately creative writing teachers have come up with ways to get past it.

First of all, it helps to remind yourself that the main purpose of your writing is to communicate your expertise and ideas, and your writing doesn't have to be perfect to achieve this. You're not perfect when you talk out loud, and you're not going to be perfect when you talk on paper. And you're not going to get any closer to writing something perfect by staring at a blank page because you're waiting for the perfect words to come to you.

When you find yourself facing a blank page, one of the best remedies is to just start typing whatever comes to mind without censoring or editing it, until you feel the ideas start to flow again. When you hear a word in your head or see it on paper, your mind automatically associates it with other words and starts a dialogue in your head. As long as you keep talking and typing, your mind will keep coming up with ideas. Eventually you'll break through the mental block you were having.

A variation on this technique is to use starter phrases to jumpstart your thought process. The starter phrases can be keywords, statements, or questions. This was the purpose of suggesting you outline your chapters and subtopics before writing your paragraphs and sentences. It gives your mind a framework to work in and expand on.

When struggling with writer's block, it's helpful to set a time slot to write down whatever comes into your head and to quit and take a break when that time is up. This gives your subconscious an opportunity to first focus on writing and then to recuperate. The time slot should vary from about 5 minutes if you're working on an outline to 20 to 40 minutes if you're writing detailed paragraphs and sentences. Don't go beyond 40 minutes without giving yourself a break for at least 10 to 15 minutes. You'll avoid burnout, and you'll give your subconscious time to relax and recover its creative energy.

What If I Still Need Help?

You might find that even after trying the techniques in this chapter, you still find writing difficult. Or you may be able to force yourself to write, but it's not enjoyable for you. Or you might decide that although you can write, if you're going to write a book showcasing your professional expertise, you'd prefer your writing to display professional quality as well.

If you're facing any of these situations, one solution is to out-source your writing to a professional ghostwriter. A ghostwriter is a writer who helps you write your book in part or in full.

When you use a ghostwriter, your name still appears on the cover of the book as the author. Sometimes the ghostwriter receives partial credit, with their name appearing under yours following designations such as "with" or "as told to." In this case the ghostwriter charges less because they receive public credit, making it easier for them to list the book in their portfolio. If the ghostwriter receives no credit on the cover, they receive more monetary compensation in return for the lost credit.

Ghostwriters vary widely in quality, so it's important to seek a good one. Reliability and skill are both important. To gauge this, it helps to find a writer with a website displaying writing samples, past clients, and testimonials.

Some ghostwriters who advertise on freelance want-ad websites like Elance hold to high standards, but most are amateurs of unpredictable quality. You'll have more luck finding a good ghostwriter by seeking a recommendation from your publisher or a writers association.

Once you've finished writing, your book is ready to begin its next stage on the way to the printers, which starts with editing.

CHAPTER 12

From the Author to the Printer

After you've filled in your outline, you have a manuscript of your book. The next stage is polishing your manuscript into a final form you can take to the printers. This stage begins with editing your text, and it includes the additional tasks of adding visual aids, laying out your pages, designing your cover, adding an index, and proofreading. In most cases the author does not handle these tasks, but the publisher delegates them to a team. Still, it helps facilitate good teamwork if the author is aware of what will happen to their manuscript between the time it leaves their hands and the time it goes to the printers, so this chapter will provide an overview of the various steps in the process.

Editing

Editing is the process of going over what you wrote and revising what needs to be rewritten. One or more editors work with the author to make sure the manuscript is thematically focused, logically well-organized, stylistically clear, factually accurate, and legally covered. In order to achieve these goals, members of the editorial team ask questions to help evaluate the manuscript and identify parts that need revision. By understanding in advance what editors will be looking for, the author can take steps to minimize the amount of revision that will be required, saving work and time both for themselves and for other members of the team.

The Author-Editor Team

If you're working with a traditional publisher, your publisher will assign your book to a professional editor with specialized training and experience. Even if you're self-publishing, it's advisable to hire an experienced editor to review your book from a detached perspective.

But although someone else will ultimately be editing your book in most cases, you as the author can still improve the efficiency of the editing process. If you know what your editor will be looking for, you can pre-edit your book as you are planning it, and you can give your first draft an editorial self-review and rewrite, minimizing the revision your editor will need to recommend.

The Goals of Editing

In professional publishing circles, the term "editing" can be used in a few different ways, and there are several different types of editing and editors. Rather than getting into technical details about job titles, let's focus on the goals common to the entire editing process. Editing aims to improve:

- Your book's overall impact
- The clarity of the flow of thought running from one chapter to the next and between the paragraphs of your chapters
- The consistency of your individual sentences with the rules of spelling, punctuation, grammar, general style guidelines, and your publisher's in-house style standards
- Factual accuracy
- Legal conformity with copyright and libel law

You may notice that the first three of these goals correspond to the structural levels you created as you were writing your manuscript. They start with the book as a whole and proceed down through your chapters and paragraphs to the level of individual sentences. Editing is essentially a matter of going back over these features of your manuscript and revising what needs to be polished up.

Question Tools to Help with Editing

To help your editor improve your book, you can use questions corresponding to the major goals of the editing process. To help edit the book's overall impact, you can ask questions such as:

- Is the book readable?
- Are the book's main points clear?
- Is the book persuasive?
- Does the book deliver the practical value promised in the title?
- Is the book emotionally engaging?

To help edit the book's flow of thought, you can ask:

- Are technical definitions introduced and defined clearly?
- Does one idea follow the next logically from chapter to chapter, subchapter to subchapter, paragraph to paragraph?
- Are there clear, smooth transitions from one major idea to the next?
- Are there any sections that should be combined or cut out?

To help edit individual sentences, ask:

- Are there any repeated spelling errors to keep an eye out for?
- Are there any repeated punctuation errors?

- Are there any repeated grammar mistakes?
- Is the style direct and clear?
- Is the style consistent with the publisher's standards? (Publishers will often provide a style sheet and/or reference a style manual.)

Finally, to help cover legal issues, the author, publisher, and their legal advisors should consider:

- Are there any quotes or visual aids that require obtaining copyright permission?
- Are there any statements about individuals posing risks of libel claims?

Tips for Making Editing Easier

Editing every line of a book sentence by sentence can take considerable time. Here are some tips to speed up the process:

- Spend some time "pre-editing" your table of contents, chapter titles, subtopics, and paragraph sequence before actually writing your paragraphs and sentences. Fixing things on these levels is much more efficient than fixing things after you've written out full sentences.
- Practice using the rules of sentence style from the last chapter until they become automatic. This will reduce the need to make revisons.
- For sections that need major rewriting, consider whether it would be more efficient to combine part of the section into another section and eliminate the rest, or even to eliminate that section altogether.

Applying these tips will make editing your book easier. Editing the text of your book is only part of the editing process, though. Before your manuscript will be ready for the printers, there are several other elements that need to be assembled, starting with visual aids.

Visual Aid Design: Tables and Illustrations

Not every book needs visual aids. But for books that do, it makes life much easier for you and your publisher if you follow certain guidelines when adding them.

Types of Visual Aids: Tables and Illustrations

Tables are textual visual aids. Tables display information in rows and columns.

Illustrations are graphic visual aids. They include photos, drawings, paintings, charts, graphs, and maps.

Guidelines for Visual Aids

Whatever type of visual aid you use, here are some guidelines to help make things easier:

- Only include as many visual aids as you need to convey vital information. Excessive visual aids can distract from your text, and visual aids add significant work and cost to production. Don't include visual aids simply for the sake of look or compulsion. Only use what you really need.
- Label tables and illustrations so that you and your layout designer are clear on which visual aid you're talking about. Tables are usually numbered as Table 1, Table 2, Table 3, etc. Illustrations are numbered in a similar way but are called Figure 1, Figure 2, Figure 3, etc.
- Use bracketed notes (called slugs) to tell your layout designer where your visual aids should go in relation to your text.
- Include labeled references (called callouts) to your visual aids in your text to let your readers know which visual aid you're talking about. Sometimes your visual aid may end up on a different page than the place in your text where you're talking about it.

- When scanning in photos and art, make sure to use the layout designer's preferred format at a sufficiently high resolution. TIFF is a generally safe format for books that will be printed physically. A good resolution for photos and gray-scale images is 300 dpi. Line art should be at least 300 but preferably 600 to 1200 dpi. Screen captures are originally 72 dpi, but after resizing, effective resolution can be 150 dpi or more.

- Keep the originals of your illustrations in separate files you can provide to your layout designer. Your layout designer will use digital publishing software to combine them with your text file later. Do not embed illustrations in the text file of your manuscript.

- Submit figure captions and legends to your publisher separately from the figures themselves. That way if your figures end up getting renumbered, you won't have to recreate them. You can insert captions and legends in the text or in a separate file.

- Make sure to secure any legal permissions you need to use others' illustrations.

If you have any questions about these or other illustration issues, ask your layout designer or publisher.

Once you've decided where your visual aids should go, your publisher will incorporate them into your layout design in the next step of the process.

Layout Design

Your book's text and visual aids come together in the layout design phase. Layout design sets up the way your pages will actually appear when printed. It aims to make your book pleasing to the eye and easy to read. As a general rule of thumb, good book design is simple, understated, and unnoticed, so that it subconsciously enhances your message rather than distracting from it.

Tasks of Layout Design

Layout places your text on your page so that it's easy to read and it fits with any visual aids you have. This involves such tasks as:

- Selecting page size (*trim*)
- Determining page length
- Considering any adjustments that will have to be made based on how the printed pages will ultimately be cut, folded, collated, and bound, along with considering the implications of any special effects such as perforation, die cutting, and embossing
- Setting up page margins
- Placing headers and footers
- Setting up columns
- Placing visual aids
- Selecting typeface

This last item alone can get quite involved, serving to illustrate the complexity of the entire process. The visual appearance of type affects the reader's emotional attitude on a subconscious level. Factors affecting this include:

- Style. Some styles of type that are easier to read on a computer screen are more difficult to read when printed. Fonts with decorative small perpendicular lines at the tips of letters (called *serif*) are harder to read on a computer screen than styles lacking this feature (called *sans serif*), but are easier to read when printed.
- Family. The same style of type can come in different families, such as regular, italic, bold, thin, condensed, expanded, shaded, etc. Some styles come in up to 20 families.
- Size. A font that's too small is hard to read, while a font that's too big is distracting. Type size measurements are not standard from one font style to the next.

- Vertical spacing between lines (*leading*). Lines that are too close or too far apart are hard to read.

- Horizontal spacing between letters. The fact that letters have different shapes requires some adjustments when spacing them out. Adjusting this includes adding space between characters (*letterspacing*), subtracting space between characters (*kerning*), and adjusting space between words (*wordspacing*).

- Line length. Lines that are too long or too short are hard to read.

- Capital letter usage. Capital letters are designed to hook the eye at the beginning of sentences and words, not to be read for entire words or lines. Overuse of capitals can strain the eye.

- Left indentation. The more zigzagging the eye has to do from one line to the next, the more the eye strains, so left indentation should be minimized.

- Right column border alignment. Whether the right border is flush (*justified*) or jagged (*unjustified*) can affect how formal or informal it looks.

- Legibility. Some fonts that are decorative are hard to read.

- Number of fonts used. Multiple typefaces confuse the eye. Using extra typefaces unnecessarily is the most common mistake amateur typesetters make.

All these factors and more must be taken into consideration by the layout designer.

Layout Design Software Requirements

Professionals normally do layout design with specialized digital publishing software. There are several reasons for using digital publishing software instead of word processing programs.

Digital publishing software creates a superior typeface appearance. Layout programs, such as InDesign and Quark, use mathematical formulas closely simulating traditional typesetting, giving the final typeface a polished appearance. This is not true of word processing programs, which use a different method of character spacing.

Layout programs are better equipped to handle illustrations than word processing programs. For best quality, illustrations should be adjusted in graphic software such as Photoshop and then imported into a layout program. Importing illustrations into a word processing program first can create problems with resolution, memory, and layout.

Layout programs also pose less risk of problems during printing. For this reason, some printers do not accept files from word-processing programs.

Layout Design Skill Requirements

As the previous discussion indicates, layout design requires specialized skills. Designers must know:

- How to use digital publishing software
- How to import text from word processing software into digital publishing software
- How to organize page margins, headers, footers, columns, and white space for a balanced appearance
- How to lay text out so it's readable
- How to import illustrations from digital software
- How to combine text and visual aids for overall impact
- How the layout will look after the book is printed and bound

Due to the extensive skill set required, it is usually best to work with a professional book designer if you want your book to have a professional appearance. Because of this, we will spare additional details and keep this discussion brief. The main point is to understand how layout design fits into the overall book production process. With this in mind, let's move on to cover design.

Cover Design

Your cover probably has more impact on your marketing than any other part of your book, so its design is crucial. Each part of your cover contributes to its marketing impact.

Qualities of a Good Cover Designer

A common mistake is to pick a cover designer simply because they have a graphic design background and their cover samples look nice. Graphic design is useful for cover design, but it is not the key to creating a marketable cover that will sell your book. Graphic design may make your cover look eye-catching and professional, but that will not in itself make your cover marketable.

To make your cover marketable, your cover design should bring your USP to life. Every aspect of your cover, including both text and graphics, should convey your USP.

To create a cover that conveys your USP, seek a cover designer who understands marketing and illustration. If they're also good at graphic design, that's a big plus, too.

Your cover designer should also know how to prepare a version of your cover the printer can use as a master, called a *book cover mechanical*. If the cover designer does not know how to do this, other members of the book production team will end up having to essentially recreate the cover file from the original design and artwork, wasting time and expense.

The Parts of Your Cover

Your USP should shine through your whole cover, with all parts supporting the overall effect. The parts of your cover include:

- The front cover
- The back cover
- The spine
- The dust jacket, if your book has one

Functions of Your Cover

The most important marketing function of your cover is to display the title. The title appears on the front cover, the spine, and the back cover. The title communicates your USP and conveys the main marketing message of your book.

The title and the rest of the front cover, along with the spine, are also particularly important for catching potential readers' attention. Colors and graphics help achieve this.

The front cover may also include a testimonial or additional information about the book's benefits.

The back cover, along with the dust jacket if there is one, can include additional information about the book's benefits, along with biographical and testimonial information establishing the author's credibility.

Versions of Your Cover

When designing your cover, bear in mind that the cover for your physical book will be larger than the version that appears online on sites such as Amazon.com. Online versions of your cover will tend to be the size of a postage stamp. Design your cover so that its most important elements will still be visible online when the size is reduced.

With your cover design complete, your book is almost ready for the printers. But there are a couple more tasks that need to be done.

Indexing and Proofreading

Your book has a couple more stops before it gets to the printers. It may need an index. And it needs proofreading. Specialists usually handle both of these tasks, so our discussion will only cover the basics needed to understand how they fit into the production process.

Indexing

Some books need indexes. An index is most helpful when your book is meant as a reference tool and it is long or complex enough that the table of contents alone is not enough to help readers locate specific information. If your book is short and simple, or if it has a purpose other than providing information, an index may not be needed.

Indexing cannot be done until after finalizing the book's interior layout and pagination, which is why it comes so late in the production process.

Simple indexing can be done automatically by a word processing program. However, a computer has no way of knowing which words are significant or how they relate to each other.

Professional indexers use specific methods to identify key words and group them together. If your index is going to be a functional reference tool for human readers and researchers, you should hire a professional indexer.

Proofreading

Proofreading is the last editorial review of your typeset manuscript (called *page proofs*) before it goes to the printers. A proofreader must review every character of every line of the book. If the proofreader misses anything, correcting it at the last minute can become involved and expensive. Proofreading is a crucial and tedious task best left to professionals.

When the proofreader is done, they submit their proposed changes to the author and publisher for approval and any final corrections. Then your book is ready for the printers!

Printing and Binding

Your proofread pages are the final version of your book before it goes to the printers. The last stage of the publishing process converts your final page proofs into a book through a two-step process: printing and binding.

Taking Your Pages to the Printers

Traditional printing uses a process called *offset printing*. In offset printing, a book's pages are photographed, and the negatives are used to make plates. The plates serve as master copies for printing reproduction. The plates are stored and reused each time the book is printed. For this process to be cost-effective, it's typically necessary to print at least 1,000 to 2,000 copies of a book, so there's usually a minimum print run requirement.

In digital printing, final page proofs are digitally converted to a file format called PDF (*Portable Document Format*). Digital presses are capable of printing one copy at a time without sacrificing cost-efficiency. This allows for what is called *print-on-demand (POD) publishing*, which has no minimum print run requirement.

Printing

Printing creates the pages of your book. The printing process differs somewhat for traditional publishers and digital publishers.

Since traditional publishers must print several thousand copies at a time to be cost-effective, the number of copies printed at one time is based on projected sales estimates, and copies are printed and stockpiled prior to actual sales. This results in 10% to 35% of books being returned to the publisher unsold, wasting money on printing, shipping, and warehousing.

Since digital publishing processes use electronically-stored PDF files as masters that afford the POD option, digital printing services can limit print runs to the number of copies necessary to keep up with actual sales. Because of this, POD publishing saves enormously on printing and other production costs.

The disadvantage of POD is that most POD publishers do not offer the same professional expertise and range of services as traditional publishers. Certain editing, production, and promotional services that would normally be handled by the publisher must be arranged by the author. Authors seeking these services from independent companies frequently encounter levels of service ranging from amateur to fraudulent. Unfortunately, first-time authors tend to lack the publishing experience to distinguish amateur operations from quality companies.

Binding

Binding attaches your pages to your cover. Binding is usually done mechanically, though it can be done in other ways. The mechanical binding process for hardcover books includes three main operations:

- *Forming* the book interior by folding printed pages, gathering them into sections, and sewing the sections together
- *Shaping* the book interior to better fit the dimensions of its cover
- *Covering* the book by creating a cover case and attaching the book to the case

Softcover books are attached to their covers by glue. Other methods of attaching books to their covers are combs, spirals, and VeloBind.

When you've finished printing and binding, congratulations! You now have a published book!

Now it's time to start promoting it.

PART IV

Announce Your Book

You've got your book written and published. Now it's time to announce your book to the world!

Publicity Goals

If you're using this book's promotional model, it's important to remember that your book is primarily a publicity tool to convey your USP. From an accounting perspective, think of the expense of publicizing your book as efficient, low-cost advertising—what professional advertisers call a "loss leader." Your book may or may not earn back some of that expense from its own sales, and may even turn a profit in its own right, but that's not the point. The point is that the book can help you reach prospects who will be interested in buying products and services that cost many times what your book costs to produce and publicize.

Because of this, the promotional strategy recommended here is not exactly the same strategy you would use to try to create a best-selling book, although there is a lot of overlap. A major publisher's goal is to sell as many copies of your book as possible in order to earn as much as possible for themselves, with you only keeping 10% to 15% or less of the profit. But the purpose of the strategy recommended in this book is not to earn profits from book sales, but to generate backend profits by getting your book into the hands of as many targeted prospects as possible. You can actually give your book away free and still earn a healthy profit, as long as a significant percentage of the prospects who read your book end up buying your products and services as a result.

Publicity Tools

So how do you get your book into the hands of targeted prospects? There are many publicity tools you can use. Rather than covering all of them, we'll focus here on a seven-pronged strategy that will establish your reputation as an expert efficiently, quickly, and cost-effectively. This strategy uses:

1. Word-of-mouth publicity: Referrals and endorsements
2. Internet and mobile phone publicity
3. Print publicity: Articles, newsletters, press releases, and book reviews
4. Digital information products: ebooks, audios, and videos
5. Speeches
6. Teaching: Seminars and coaching
7. Interviews

We'll also discuss how to follow your initial publicity push so that once you get in the limelight, you stay there.

CHAPTER 13

Word-of-Mouth Publicity: Referrals and Endorsements

Word-of-mouth publicity is the most effective form of publicity, and also the most neglected by traditional advertising consultants. Referrals from satisfied customers are the most persuasive form of advertising and the least expensive. Endorsements from recognized experts and celebrities can carry similar weight. These two tools should form the foundation of your publicity campaign.

Referrals

Most business is generated by referrals from satisfied customers. But few marketing consultants know how to generate referrals, and they either overlook their significance or assume they occur by chance. There are ways to systematically increase your referral rate. Here are some simple but effective strategies:

- Set standards of customer service using specific categories and measurements, and monitor customer feedback to make sure you are meeting those standards. For example, "How would you rate our staff's friendliness on a scale of 1 to 5?"
- Train yourself and your employees to meet your standards of customer service.

- Establish rapport with new prospects by formally welcoming them and focusing on their experiences and needs.
- Tell prospects about your standards of service and encourage them to complain when those standards are not met.
- Tell new prospects about previous satisfied clients, so that they will remember this information when they talk to others about you.
- Overdeliver by providing more than the customer expects and more than you promised.
- Send customers thank-yous.
- Give customers surprise gifts.
- Ask for customer feedback and advice.
- Seek out complaints and respond to them.
- Ask customers to test-market new products and services.
- Ask for referrals and create programs to reward customers who bring referrals.
- Identify the customers who generate the most referrals, pay special attention to them, and provide them with additional information to pass on to others.
- Dramatically illustrate customers making referrals in your promotions and advertisements.

You can apply these strategies to generate referrals for your book in some specific ways:

- Tell current customers about your book. Send out a promotional postcard or email. Consider offering a discounted or free copy of the book and/or another product or service.
- Tell past customers in your database about your book.
- Create incentives for customers to tell others about your book.

Getting your customers to talk to others about your book is probably the easiest way to promote it effectively.

Endorsements

You can think of endorsements as a special type of referral, coming from recognized experts in your field and from celebrities. Endorsements can provide powerful testimonials to include on your book cover, in your book's front matter, and in your promotional and sales literature.

How do you obtain endorsements? If you already know an expert in your field or a celebrity, you can ask them if they would be willing to contribute a quote or foreword. If you don't know any experts or celebrities, there are several types of resources you can use to find them:

- Directories of experts and celebrities are published periodically and may be available through reference libraries. There are also online expert directories. Useful online resources include ExpertClick, Experts.com, and PRNewswire's ProfNet service.

- Directories of professional organizations related to your subject area may provide contact information for experts. You can also join such organizations and network through them.

- Educational institutions, corporations, and government agencies may be willing to suggest experts in a given field. Matthew Lesko's books and websites are a valuable resource for finding experts through government agencies.

- You can draw names from authors of existing books and articles written about your subject area. Children's nonfiction books and encyclopedias are particularly good resources for locating top experts quickly. Contact information for authors is sometimes available online or in biographical references on authors. It is also possible to contact authors through their publishers.

- Public figures and celebrities may have press secretaries or publicists who can be used to contact them.

Once you've located someone to endorse your book, how do you go about persuading them to do so? If you already have a relationship with them through friendship or correspondence, the subject may arise naturally through conversation. For someone you don't know, you may write them a letter asking them to review an advance copy of your book. If you suspect they may be too busy to read your entire book, you might put together a shorter excerpt for them to review.

If you can obtain endorsements before printing your book, you can use them in your book. Otherwise you can use them in your promotional and sales literature, and save them for future editions of your book.

Referrals and endorsements give you a solid foundation to build on when you branch off into other parts of your promotional campaign. They provide you with testimonials you can use in other media, such as the Internet and mobile phones, which are our next subject.

CHAPTER 14

Internet and Mobile Phone Publicity

The Internet and mobile phones have become hot trends in publicity today. Some businesses center their promotional efforts around these new tools.

However, as with any fad, these tools have not replaced proven methods. They work best when you combine them with traditional tools together into a single, integrated, focused strategy.

Here we will describe an integrated Internet and mobile phone publicity strategy adopted from direct mail marketing. The principles underlying this strategy have been proven to work effectively both offline and online.

Borrowing a Proven Direct Marketing Strategy

Direct mail marketers have found that one of the most effective sales strategies is to build an in-house mailing list by giving away free information. This strategy may be applied online in conjunction with mobile phone marketing.

Free information offers attract prospects who are interested in your type of product or service, ensuring that you are not wasting advertising efforts on people outside your target market. When these prospects contact you, you gain the opportunity to place them on a mailing list of prospective customers. Studies have shown that prospective customers who do not buy from you immediately may often buy from you if you follow up with half a dozen or more efforts to contact them. Once they have bought from you, you may now add them to a mailing list of customers who have purchased from you, known as an *in-house mailing list*. Research has proven that you have better odds of selling something to customers on your in-house mailing list than to new prospects. This is because your in-house customers have already been persuaded to buy from you, so much of your sales work has already been done.

Applying the Strategy Online and with Mobile Phones

This direct marketing strategy may be integrated with Internet and mobile phone tools. Internet and mobile phone tools can be used in conjunction with traditional tools to promote free information offers and attract prospects to a mailing list. Prospects proceed through a sequence of steps called a *sales funnel*, designed to guide them through the process of becoming a customer.

The sales funnel sequence includes these general steps:

1. Free information is offered to prospects through a variety of tools, which can encompass traditional media, Internet media, and mobile phone marketing. The free information offer includes contact information directing the customer to a special web page called a "squeeze page."

2. Prospects who respond to the free information offer are directed to the squeeze page. The squeeze page offers free information in exchange for the prospect's email contact information. The free information often takes the form of an electronic newsletter or free PDF report. A digital form called an *opt-in form* is supplied for the prospect to submit their name and email address.

3. Once the prospect fills in the opt-in form, their contact information is added to an electronic mailing list database. The database is managed by an automated mailing list manager, called an *autoresponder*. An autoresponder service charges a monthly fee that allows you to mail all members of your mailing list at once, as often as you like, without additional cost. You can send out one-time broadcasts announcing special news, or program the autoresponder to space a sequence of prewritten messages out over time according to a prearranged schedule.

4. Your autoresponder allows you to continue providing your prospects with free information on an ongoing basis, and in the process make periodic commercial offers. The free information sustains your prospects' awareness of you and your relationship with them. Commercial offers can be included in regular electronic newsletters (also called "e-zines") or issued separately as solo promotions.

5. Prospects who have responded to your offers by purchasing can be placed on an in-house mailing list to be used for specific follow-up promotions.

Following these steps properly maximizes your odds of moving prospects through your sales funnel and converting them into customers.

Putting the Strategy into Practice Step-by-Step

Putting this strategy into practice is probably most easily approached and explained by starting at the end of the sales funnel and building it backwards. Now this is not the only way to do it. Theoretically it is possible to start building any part of the sales funnel first. But this way works and is easy to use if you're starting from scratch:

1. Create an offer, including a product or service and a supporting sales page.

2. Write an autoresponder email sequence to promote the offer. The sequence should include free giveaway information, such as an electronic newsletter, as well as the offer itself. If you are going to give away a free PDF report, you would also need to create or acquire this.

3. Create an autoresponder account and mailing list and upload your email sequence into the list.

4. Create a squeeze page and opt-in form for your website. If you do not have a website you will also need to build one. This involves acquiring a domain name, setting up a hosting service, designing your webpages, and placing your webpages on your site. Your website should at a minimum include a few important pages and features: a home page with a general greeting, a contact information page, legal pages disclosing your privacy policy and terms of use, and a site map to help search engines index your site.

5. Promote your website by issuing free information offers using traditional, Internet, and mobile phone media tools.

Tools for Putting the Strategy into Effect

As indicated, this strategy can be implemented with a combination of traditional, Internet, and mobile phone media tools.

Traditional tools include print, radio, and TV publicity and advertising methods. You can use any of these to promote your website. For instance, you can run a classified newspaper ad giving a link to your website for more information.

Internet tools you can use to promote your website include:

- Your autoresponder mailing lists.
- Free articles archived on your site.
- Membership areas of your site accessible by subscription only, either through free sign-up or for a periodic fee.

- Free newsletters archived on your site.

- Blog posts on your site.

- Guest blog posts and visitor comments on other blogs which allow you to include a direct or indirect link back to your site. You can sometimes link back to your site directly in your comment, and sometimes indirectly through a profile.

- Forum posts and comments on sites which allow you to link back to your site.

- Posts on sites devoted to answering frequently asked questions that allow you to link back to your site. A popular frequently-asked-question site is Yahoo! Answers (http://answers.yahoo.com).

- Book review comments on online bookseller sites allowing you to link back to your site. The most popular online bookseller is Amazon.com.

- Article posts on sites allowing you to link back to your site. Ezine (http://ezinearticles.com) is the leading general article site.

- Video posts on sites allowing you to link back to your site. YouTube (http://www.youtube.com) is the leading video site.

- Social media posts back to your site. Popular social media include Facebook (http://www.facebook.com), Twitter (http://twitter.com), MySpace (http://www.myspace.com), and LinkedIn (http://www.linkedin.com).

- Search engine optimization (SEO). This is a method of matching the keywords emphasized on your site's pages to keywords that are popular search topics on search engines such as Google, Yahoo!, and Bing. Ideal keywords have high search volume, a low number of competing websites, a low page rank for competing websites, and high advertising revenue as indicated by the amount of money bid for corresponding online ad space.

- Affiliate marketing. Affiliate marketing is recruiting a business ally, called a *joint venture partner* (*JV partner*), to promote your site or offer to their mailing list in return for some compensation, such as a commission or a cross-promotion to your list.
- Online press releases.
- Online book reviews of your book by third-party reviewers.
- Online seminars, called *webinars*.
- Online coaching programs.
- Online interviews.
- Online classified advertising. Some free and commercial software tools allow you to submit classified ads to a large number of sites at once without paying a per-ad fee.
- Online paid advertising. This is the most costly and risky method listed here and should not be pursued without professional assistance. It is easy to lose a lot of money very quickly using this method.

Mobile phone tools often work in conjunction with Internet tools. For instance, a high search ranking on Google can help your business show up on top when a mobile phone user searches for businesses in your industry in their geographic area.

A number of the tools mentioned above fall into categories overlapping with other promotional tools that will be covered in the following chapters. Articles, one of the most basic and useful tools, will be covered next, along with some other print publicity tools.

CHAPTER 15

Print Publicity: Articles, Newsletters, Press Releases, and Book Reviews

"Print publicity" these days includes both traditional and online "print," and both types are included here. Whether you're offline or online, the process of print publicity involves:

1. Creating publicity pieces
2. Distributing them

Types of Print Publicity

Your book is itself a form of print publicity. Other key forms that are effective for promoting your book are:

- Articles
- Newsletters
- Press releases
- Book reviews

Let's talk about how to write each of these and how to distribute them.

Articles

Articles are a way to reach targeted prospects with an excerpt of your book's message and a plug for your book. You can begin publicizing your book with articles even before your book is released.

Writing Articles

Writing an article is a lot like writing a chapter of your book. Two important differences are that you have less editorial control over an article, and an article must stand alone without the support of other chapters.

As when writing your book, it's important to start writing your article by doing market research. Find out what important publications or websites are popular in your field, what topics their readers are interested in, and what other writers are saying about those topics. Some good tools for collecting this information are:

- Periodical directories and indexes, found in your library's reference section.
- *Writer's Market*, found in library reference sections and bookstore writing sections.
- Google Reader, found online (www.google.com/reader). Use the "Add a Subscription" option to sign up for syndicated news feeds about a keyword phrase. You can save time reading by selecting "All items," which will display headline summaries of your news feeds.
- Ezine Articles, found online (http://ezinearticles.com).

Use your market research to pick a topic. The topic should be a topic you can use to point readers to your book for more information. You will save writing time if you can tie the topic into topics already covered in your book. You may be able to create an article by making minor changes to a chapter of your book.

The process of writing an article is similar to the process of writing a book chapter. Start with a title and outline and work your way down to individual paragraphs. Here is a good method for writing articles:

1. Name your title, using the same principles you used to name your book.

2. Outline your article. Include an introductory paragraph, at least three main points, and a concluding paragraph.

3. Write your introductory paragraph first to set the tone of your article. Include an attention-getting opening, a sentence stating your theme, and a sentence or bulleted list summarizing what topics you intend to cover. Your opening sentences can attract attention by posing a question, providing some information, making a statement, starting an argument, identifying a need, offering a benefit, or telling a story.

4. Write your concluding paragraph next, so you know what you're building towards in the rest of your article. Include a recap of your main point and a concluding sentence encouraging your reader to take some action. The action you ultimately want them to take is to consult your book for more information, but since most publishers won't let you directly plug your book in the body of your article, it's better to indirectly suggest some course of action that logically encourages readers to consult your book.

5. Fill in your body paragraphs.

6. Add a brief biographical statement identifying you as the author of your book. Include your book's website if you have one and if the publication you are submitting to allows it.

The length of your article will depend on the policy of the publication where you intend to publish it.

Distributing Articles

After you've written an article, where do you publish it? The same sources recommended for market research double as sources for article distribution. *Writer's Market* and Ezine (http://ezinearticles.com) are two of the best places to start. Online, you can also post your articles to blogs, social media, and forums and syndicate them through RSS feeds. If you are targeting a local geographic area, you can publish in local newspapers and other local and regional publications.

When submitting an article for distribution, be sure to study the publication's submission guidelines. Some traditional periodicals will prefer a query letter.

Newsletters

Your articles can be collected into newsletter format. A newsletter is an excellent way to maintain regular contact with prospects and customers. You can include offers for products and services in your newsletter. You can even sell ad space.

In addition to including your own articles in your newsletter, you can ask other contributors to submit original articles. You can also find articles with limited reprint rights on sites such as Ezine (http://ezinearticles.com).

Newsletters can be distributed both through the mail and online. If you have a traditional mailing list of prospects or customers, you can mail your newsletter to your list. You can also create an electronic mailing list by adding an opt-in form to your website and using your autoresponder service to distribute your newsletter.

Press Releases

A cost-effective way to promote your book is to send out press releases announcing your book's publication or other associated events. A press release is a news item announcing some news related to your book, such as:

- Your book's publication.

- The release of a new edition.
- A public appearance by the author.
- An award received by the author.
- Public service information. For instance, you may summarize material from your book by providing readers with a free sample of expert tips on your subject, and in the process you can mention your book by referring to yourself as the author, by referencing your book for additional information, or by offering copies of your book.

Writing Press Releases

Here are some guidelines for writing effective press releases:

- A press release should include a header providing your name and contact information, your recipient's name and address, and the date of the press release.
- Editors will often condense your press release to meet space requirements, so position important information and adjust your length accordingly. Be sure to put essential information in the first sentence. Ideally aim to fit your release on a standard 8.5" x 11" sheet of paper. (Note that because our book is smaller than a regular sheet of paper, our example appears larger.)
- The tone of a press release should sound like you're announcing news, not advertising a product, so avoid sales language. However, if applicable, do give essential details about your book, such as price and how it may be purchased.
- A press release stands a better chance of being printed if it focuses on a newsworthy event or information associated with the author of a book, rather than on the book itself.

See the following page for a sample illustrating the format of a press release.

Sample Press Release

FROM:

John Dough

Debt into Dollars

666 Fifth Avenue, Suite 4200

New York, NY 10065

1-800-123-4567

http://www.debtintodough.com/

For more information, please contact Mr. Dough at
1-800-123-4567.

FOR:

[Name of recipient]

[Address]

[City, State Zip]

FOR IMMEDIATE RELEASE

[Date]

###

Millionaire author offers free tips on "How to Turn Debt into Dollars"

On Wednesday June 16, 2010, millionaire debt relief expert John
Dough will offer free tips from his new book *How to Turn Debt*

into Dollars. The speech will be held in the Manhattan Chamber of Commerce, 1375 Broadway, Third Floor at 7:00 PM and is free to the general public.

"Debt collection is the one industry where anyone can make money no matter how badly the economy is doing, and anyone can learn to do it with a weekend of training," Dough explains in his book.

The speech will cover where to find debt collection opportunities, how to evaluate them, how to win bids, how to secure complete financing without spending your own money, and how to collect payments without hassles.

For more information or to arrange interviews or appearances, contact Mr. Dough at 1-800-123-4567.

###

Distributing Press Releases

For a fee, you can have your press release sent to wide range of outlets by using the services of various agencies, such as:

- GAP Enterprises' Automated Press Releases: http://www.automatedpr.com
- Press Release Network: http://www.pressreleasenetwork.com/index.html
- ProfNet, Inc.: http://www.profnet.org/index.html

Email news release services targeting online readers include both commercial and free services, such as:

- 24-7 Press Release: http://www.24-7pressrelease.com
- ArticleCity Press Release Distribution Network: http://articlecity.prwebdirect.com
- BookCatcher: http://www.bookcatcher.com
- eReleases: http://www.ereleases.com
- ExpertClick.com NewsReleaseWire.com: http://www.expertclick.com/NewsReleaseWire
- InternetNews: http://www.internetnews.com
- Majon International: http://www.majon.com/advanced/advanced-pr.html
- The Open Press: http://www.theopenpress.com
- PR Leap: http://www.prleap.com
- PRWeb Press Release Newswire: http://www.prwebdirect.com
- PR.com: http://www.pr.com/press-releases
- Send2Press: http://www.send2press.com
- Xpress Press: http://www.xpresspress.com

Book Reviews

Another cost-effective print publicity method is book reviews. Positive book reviews increase your credibility by providing testimony from third parties. Even negative book reviews can attract attention by generating controversy.

Types of Book Reviews

Book reviews fall into two categories: pre-publication and post-publication.

In traditional publishing, pre-publication reviews are based on your galleys (early copies of your book that may not yet be fully proofread or bound) and must be received by reviewers three or four months before your book's official publication date (which is actually three or four months after your book comes off the press). With print-on-demand publishing, this schedule may be more flexible. Pre-publication reviews are generally focused on major or key reviewers.

Post-publication review packages can be sent out at any time to a broader range of reviewers.

Preparing Book Review Packages

When sending out a galley or review copy of your book, in addition to your book itself, it is recommended to include supplementary material which summarizes essential information for reviewers. One of the most important items to include is a sheet attached to your book's inside cover, summarizing your book's vital data:

- Title
- Author
- Publisher

- Publisher's contact information
- ISBN
- Price
- Publishing date

In addition to this vital data sheet, other items you can consider including are:

- A press release
- An author biography
- Select excerpts
- A mock review

Distributing Book Reviews

Who should you send your review package to? Your book will get the most effective reviews if you can contact the leading reputation builders in your field. These fall into several sometimes overlapping categories:

- Opinion leaders. These are leaders who shape public opinion in a field by following trends, buying new products early, and airing their opinions to a wide audience.
- Market trend watchers. These are commentators on market trends who dispense consumer advice about where to shop for the best products, services, and prices.
- Product and service reviewers. These are enthusiasts who display a hobbyist's interest in purchasing and comparing products and services.
- Social trend-setters. These are cultural connoisseurs who like to be close to the latest social trends and influence their direction.

Reviews from these types of reputation builders can have an exponential impact on publicity. You should identify the reputation builders in your field and send them review packages for your book. Companies such as R.R. Bowker provide services such as BookWire which will assist you in reaching reviewers for a fee. You can also cultivate your own list of potential reviewers by using resources available in libraries and online, such as:

- General directories of media contacts, such as Bacon's *MediaSource, MediaLists Online,* and *Internet Media Directory;* Gebbie Press' *All-In-One Media Directory;* and NewsLink.

- Directories of newspapers. When contacting newspapers, you may sometimes have more luck approaching feature and Sunday editors than departmental editors. Some major directories include *Bacon's Newspaper/Media Directory, Editor & Publisher,* NewsVoyager, PubList.com, and *Working Press of the Nation, Volume 1: Newspaper Directory.*

- Directories of consumer magazines and trade journals. Standard Rate and Data Service publishes *Consumer Magazine* and *Business Publications* directories, which are particularly useful.

- Directories of newsletters. Consult the *Oxbridge Directory of Newsletters. Working Press of the Nation* also has a useful volume on *Internal Publications,* covering internal employee newsletters.

- Directories of professional associations. You can find these listed in Thomson Gale's *Encyclopedia of Associations* (EA) and *Encyclopedia of Associations: Internal Organizations* (IO), *The National Trade and Professional Association Directory,* or online directories such as associationcentral.com or the Internet Public Library's *Associations on the Net* page.

- Other specialized directories.

Beyond reviewers specific to your industry, there are also general book reviewers you may wish to contact, depending on your market. Major pre-publication reviewers include:

- *Booklist* (library books): http://www.ala.org/ala/aboutala/offices/publishing/ booklist_publications/booklist/booklist.cfm

- *ForeWord Reviews* (independent press- and university press-published books): http://www.forewordreviews.com
- *Independent Publisher* (independently-published books): http://www.independentpublisher.com
- *Kirkus Reviews*: http://www.kirkusreviews.com kirkusreviews/index.jsp
- *Library Journal* (library books): http://www.libraryjournal.com
- *New York Review of Books*: http://www.nybooks.com
- *New York Times Book Review*: http://www.nytimes.com/pages/books
- *Publishers Weekly*: http://www.publishersweekly.com
- *Quill & Quire*: http://www.quillandquire.com
- *Washington Post Book World*: http://www.washington-post.com/wp-dyn/content/print/bookworld/index.html

Articles, press releases, and book reviews form the foundation of a powerful print publicity campaign. Articles can also be reformatted and leveraged into other types of publicity.

CHAPTER 16

Digital Information Products: Ebooks, Audios, and Videos

Articles can be spun off into digital information products. These include:

- Ebooks
- Audios
- Videos

The methods of creating and distributing these are similar to those for articles, with some distinctions unique to each medium.

Ebooks

Ebooks are PDF publications distributed online. Depending on their length, frequency, format, and purpose, they can also be called special reports, white papers, handbooks, newsletters, etc.

Creating Ebooks

An easy way to write an ebook is to collect material from your book and your articles into an original package. You can also use other writings from your archives, write a new ebook about a marketable topic, find public domain material to reprint, interview other experts, or recruit expert contributors.

The length of your ebook can vary from 10 pages to hundreds of pages. Research has determined that 69 to 80 pages is ideal to establish credibility without getting too lengthy.

After writing your ebook in a word processing program, you can save it as a PDF file. You should also create a cover image to display on webpages promoting your ebook. The cover image does not necessarily have to appear in the ebook itself, though it can.

Distributing Ebooks

You can distribute an ebook from your own website, from others' websites, through others' mailing lists, or through electronic devices such as an Amazon Kindle.

Others who assist you in distributing ebooks are known as *joint venture partners (JV partners)*. In return for distributing your ebooks, JV partners will usually expect a commission, cross-promotional use of your mailing list, or some other reward.

Short ebooks are often given away free as loss leaders. They are typically offered as an incentive to sign up for a mailing list, which is then used to promote higher-priced products and services.

When sold to consumers, longer ebooks generally sell in the $20 to $50 range. When sold to businesses, they can sell anywhere from $97 to $1,500.

Audios

Information packaged in ebook format can also be packaged in audio format. Audios can be faster to produce than other information products. They can be distributed independently or in conjunction with supplementary products.

Creating Audios

An audio can have the same essential format as an article and take the form of a narrated article. It can also be a recording of an interview, speech, seminar, or drama.

The minimal requirement for creating an audio is a recording device. Sound quality can be improved by using specialized input devices such as microphones and headphones, and by using audio editing software.

Audios are stored as digital files. Lengthy audios can be broken up into multiple files.

Distributing Audios

Audios can be distributed in physical format as CDs, or electronically through the same channels as ebooks. They can also be distributed through video distribution channels by adding a visual still shot or other visual element to accompany the sound.

Audios can be distributed free as loss leaders, or they can be sold for $47 to $97 and up.

Videos

Information from ebook and audio format can also be packaged in video format. Videos can be generated by slideshows, live photography, or animation. They allow visual effects to be used and combined with audio effects. Like audios, they can be distributed independently or in conjunction with supplementary products.

Creating Videos

Videos can take an information-oriented format similar to an ebook or audio. They can also take a more dramatic format similar to a movie, TV show, or commercial.

The easiest way to create a video is to create a slideshow presentation. The presentation can be silent or it can be narrated.

Video can also be created from live photography or animation.

Audio soundtrack for videos can be recorded in two ways. The easiest way is to record it live while the video is being filmed, but this requires well-rehearsed timing. To make synchronization more manageable, audio can be recorded as a separate track and combined with the accompanying video track later in a video editing program.

Video editing programs also allow various special effects to be added to videos, such as animation, captions, and frame transitions.

Distributing Videos

Videos can be distributed physically as CDs or DVDs, or electronically through video hosts, distribution networks, and services. The most important online video host is currently YouTube (http://www.youtube.com). Important distribution networks and services include TubeMogul (http://www.tubemogul.com) and Traffic Geyser (http://www.trafficgeyser.com).

Ebooks, audios, and videos can promote your book independently or in conjunction with each other as bundled packages. In addition to promoting your book directly, they can also be used to transcribe or record your public speaking promotional events, which form the remaining prongs of your promotional strategy.

CHAPTER 17

Speeches

The same information that you record in digital format can also be delivered live. You can deliver it in person in the traditional manner, over the phone through a teleconference, or over the Internet through a webinar. Whichever format you use, similar principles of preparation apply.

Preparing for Speeches

Many people are almost as afraid of public speaking as they are of death. Fortunately, most of this fear stems from lack of preparation, and it can be remedied by following some simple steps:

- Practice relaxing. Use visual and auditory cues, progressive muscle relaxation, and deep breathing to train your body to relax. Practice conditioning yourself to go into a relaxed state, so that you can relax before your speech.

- Research your audience. Find out as much as you can about who they are, what they already know about your topic, and what they're interested in hearing about.

- Plan your speech. You can use the same writing techniques you used to plan your book and articles. Outline your main points. But instead of writing down individual sentences, only jot down key details you need to remember. Don't try to memorize everything, just the essentials. The less you have to memorize, the less anxiety you will experience.

- Rehearse. You can practice speaking to the air, to a mirror, into a microphone, to a friend, and to a small group of friends. Each practice will build your confidence.

- Open your speech with a strong entrance. Plan your opening to build a relationship with your audience, get their attention, and arouse their interest.

- Use body language effectively. Stand in a relaxed position, remaining relatively stationary. Only walk around or gesture when it helps dramatize your point. To maintain eye contact with your audience, pick one audience member on the left side of the room, one in the middle, and one on the right for visual reference.

- Close your speech by recapping your main points and indicating what action your audience should take.

With respect to the last point, your closing should steer your audience towards reading your book.

Getting Public Speaking Engagements

How do you get public speaking engagements? There are several major ways, some involving traditional methods, some using online opportunities:

- Use local networking to promote a speaking event. Local promotional allies can include businesses, conventions, your Chamber of Commerce, libraries, educational institutions, churches, charities, fraternal societies, and service clubs.

- Use public speaking associations and bureaus to help you. The National Speakers Association and National Speakers Bureau are good resources to start with.

- Organize a teleconference using a website, mailing list, and online business allies.
- Organize a webinar using the same online tools.

When arranging a speaking engagement, it's a good idea to contact your host first to test audience interest in potential topics.

You can use your speaking engagements both for publicity and as practice for teaching and interview opportunities, which we will discuss next.

CHAPTER 18

Teaching: Seminars and Coaching

Speaking is good practice for teaching, which is another way to promote your book. Teaching involves speaking, but adds more interaction with your audience. The size of the group and the style of the presentation divide teaching into different formats, such as seminars and coaching, each of which can be delivered in both face-to-face and online formats.

Whichever format you use, certain principles are key to success. Here we will cover:

- Types of teaching formats
- How to plan teaching presentations
- How to organize teaching events
- How to deliver teaching events
- How to book teaching events
- How to promote teaching events
- How to use teaching events to promote your book

Types of Teaching Formats

Teaching formats can vary in several different ways. Variables include the size of the group, the style of interaction, and whether the format is live or online.

Teaching formats for small to medium-sized groups include seminars and workshops. Teaching formats for very small groups and individuals include coaching and consulting.

Styles of interaction vary from one format to another. A seminar tends to be like a lecture, with an emphasis on information. A workshop is more like a lab, with an emphasis on hands-on application. Other formats include symposiums, colloquiums, training programs, clinics, bootcamps, retreats, conferences, and masterminds.

Any of these formats can be conducted face-to-face or online. Face-to-face formats allow better body language interaction and physical demonstrations. Online formats allow more flexible use of audiovisual aids and instant group communication.

The discussion here will address face-to-face events, focusing on seminars as a typical example. If you are using another format or teaching online, you should find it easy to adapt what is said here to your format.

Planning Teaching Presentations

Planning your presentation is similar to planning your book. Like your book, your seminar should aim to bring specific benefits to a specific target market. Ideally, you can actually have your audience help you select your seminar's topics. One way to do this is to send potential hosts or attendees a questionnaire. Make a list of about ten topics you can tie into your book. Ask your prospective audience to pick their top three preferences from the list, and then to pick which of these they'd most want covered if only one was available. You can then organize your presentation around the top picks, assigning time slots to each topic and giving priority to requested topics.

Organize your presentation so that your information is presented logically, clearly, and in chunks small enough for your audience to absorb, with enough repetition and application to facilitate retention. Here are some principles to help you organize your presentation:

- Plan to start with an introductory segment to establish a relationship with your audience. Break the ice, introduce yourself, introduce seminar participants to each other, tell your audience where restrooms and phones are available, and mention any refreshments that are available. If your audience is up to 25 people, each member can introduce themselves. Otherwise you can have them break into small groups and introduce themselves to other members of their group.

- As a follow-up to your introduction, ask your audience questions about their needs and concerns to get them participating from the beginning. Structure your presentation to encourage audience participation. Use methods such as group questions, quizzes, pairing activities, small group discussions, and games.

- Use an outline to facilitate your audience's understanding and retention.

- Break information up into small, digestible chunks. Allot time to reinforce each chunk through illustrations, repetition, and practice.

- Schedule breaks between major chunks.

Hold audience attention by spicing up the factual side of your presentation with stories, quotes, and humor.

- Use visual aids when appropriate.

- Design handouts that support your presentation without distracting from it. Be aware that if you pass material out while you are still talking, some members of your audience will end up reading it instead of listening to you, so anything you pass out should complement what you say aloud and be passed out in timing with what you have to say. Handouts can include name tags, outlines, quizzes, resource lists, evaluation forms, promotional literature, and sign-up sheets for your mailing list.

- Be sure to bring pencils or pens if your audience will need to write anything on their handouts.
- Include contact information in your handouts in case participants wish to contact you later about ordering your book or scheduling you for other seminars.

Practice your presentation ahead of time, as you would a speech. Record yourself so you can work on your voice and measure the length of your talk. Use a mirror to practice your posture, facial expressions, and body language. Test your presentation on friends. If you want to improve your speaking skills, professional speaking organizations can provide training resources.

In addition to planning your presentation, you will need to organize the event itself.

Organizing Teaching Events

A key part of organizing your seminar is selecting the location and time.

The location should be accessible to your target market and within the means of your target market. Getting an organization to sponsor your seminar may enable you to choose a more expensive location than you could afford to rent yourself. The selected facility should be able to provide whatever you require by way of space, seating, audiovisual equipment, and food and beverage service.

The date should not conflict with major vacation periods, holidays, or other national events. Tuesday through Thursday are generally the best days to give seminars. Fridays can also work well for seminars sponsored by businesses, since the seminar effectively becomes the first day of a three-day weekend for employees. Sunday and Monday are bad days for seminars.

Half-day seminars are best scheduled either during the first half of the business day before lunch, from lunch to the close of first shift, or long enough after the supper hour that attendees have a chance to eat and travel before the seminar starts. (6:30 PM to 9:30 PM is a good time frame.) Afternoon and full-day seminars should end early enough to give participants a jump on rush-hour traffic.

Be sure to allow time for breaks, question-and-answer sessions, and meals. Audience concentration tends to dwindle if a presentation goes longer than 40 to 50 minutes without a break.

Be sure to confirm your room reservation. It is a good idea to get this confirmation in writing by creating a form that itemizes the details of your reservation requirements and fees. Include lines for:

- The contact information of the individual and organization providing your room.
- The date and time of the meeting.
- The name of your seminar (to be listed on forms and signs).
- The number of attendees you will be expecting.
- How you want the room set up. (You can include a diagram depicting seat/table arrangements.)
- The name/number of the room you will be using (if applicable).
- Requested audiovisual equipment.
- Requested water service.
- Requested food/beverage service.
- Itemized fees and total fee for room rental, audiovisual rental, water service, and food/beverage service.

As we will discuss later, you can offer a seminar for free or for a fee depending on the circumstances. If you're going to charge for your seminar, you should set your price so that your seminar is affordable to your audience, competitive with your competition, and profitable to you.

Your profit will be a product of the fee per participant times the number of participants, so it can be worth your while to test-market how your number of participants varies with different prices offered.

If another organization is sponsoring your seminar, they may play a role in determining how many participants attend and how much you are paid. The fee a sponsoring organization is willing to pay will tend to vary with the type of organization involved. As a general rule, corporations tend to pay more, educational institutions tend to pay less.

Offering discounts to early registrants and groups can increase participation.

Measure your bottom line by the ratio of how much you earn per dollar spent on promoting your seminar. A return of $3 for every $1 spent on promotion is considered good in the seminar business; a return of $4 for every $1 is great. If you are doing the seminar as a free promotion, you should measure the profitability of the seminar in terms of how your promotional expenses weigh against income generated from attendees who become customers. You can track this as a ratio over time.

If an organization is sponsoring your seminar, require a prepaid deposit to hold the speaking date. Otherwise you risk wasted time and money if they cancel.

Delivering Teaching Events

Try to arrive early so you can make sure the room is ready and be prepared to greet your guests. Ideally, it's advisable to visit the seminar site the day before so you can make an on-the-spot inspection. You may need to check things such as signs, seating, tables, audiovisual equipment, lighting, temperature, names and location of staff, location of restroom facilities and telephones, location of drinking fountains, availability of water and cups, and other food and beverage arrangements. You may wish to distribute some handouts before your audience arrives.

If someone will be introducing you to your audience, you should discuss what they will say ahead of time. Have a typed introduction ready to give them. Ask them to conclude by mentioning that personally autographed copies of your book are available at a table.

Build time into your presentation to direct attention to the table where your book is available. This can be done during transitions to breaks and at other key points when appropriate. Make sure your audience is aware your book is available, but do not overemphasize this during your presentation.

At the conclusion of your presentation, be sure to summarize your key points and thank your audience and anyone who assisted in your presentation. End with a call challenging your audience to some concrete action applying the information they have just learned. End on time. Practice your conclusion ahead of time.

Booking Teaching Events

There are three major ways to book teaching events:

- Organize and promote them yourself.
- Find a sponsor.
- Hire a public seminar provider.

Organizations which sponsor seminars include educational institutions (especially continuing educational institutions), professional associations, trade associations, corporations, government agencies, and religious institutions.

Leading public seminar providers include:

- Fred Pryor Seminars & Career Track: http://www.career-track.com/site/default.aspx
- The Learning Annex: http://www.learningannex.com

If you're trying to persuade an organization to sponsor your seminar, you should ask them if they have a budget for speakers. Finding out what this budget is can help you set your asking price.

Make sure you get any agreements with your sponsor in writing, including details about the name and topic of your seminar, the length of your presentation, what expenses your sponsor is covering, whether your sponsor is buying any copies of your book for attendees, and your right to sell your book and other products and distribute your own promotional literature at the seminar. Some sponsors will not agree to allow you to sell products or promote yourself at a seminar they are sponsoring. Some sponsors may ask permission to videotape your presentation for reference or to provide or sell to members of their organization unable to attend. If you agree to this, be sure you retain rights to a master copy of the tape and rights to sell your own copies of the tape. Get this agreement in writing.

If you find a sponsor for your seminar, they will usually help you promote it.

Promoting Teaching Events

An effective promotional tactic is to offer a free or low-cost introductory seminar followed up by a more expensive advanced seminar. Your introductory seminar should give away enough useful information to deliver value to your audience and attract their interest, but not so much information that they don't need your advanced seminar. You can use both the introductory seminar and the follow-up as opportunities to distribute your book.

Another promotional tactic is to offer free copies of your book or other materials to a set number of people who register for your seminar first.

Depending on your budget, direct mail and paid advertising may also be useful.

Using Teaching Events to Promote Your Book

Your seminar should offer copies of your book either as a free giveaway or for sale.

You will increase distribution of your book if you find a way to put a copy of your book in the hands of each participant, rather than just waiting for them to come to a book table. One way to do this is to place a copy of the book at each participant's seat so they have an opportunity to examine it for themselves. You could work your book into your seminar presentation as a way of encouraging them to do this. You may also include an opportunity to buy your book at a discount when attendees register for the seminar. If an organization is sponsoring your seminar, you may be able to convince them to buy a copy of your book for each participant at a discounted rate.

Whatever other means you use to distribute your book, you should include a book table, in case anyone wants extra copies. To increase the effectiveness of your book table, you can:

- Make sure the table is visible. Placing it somewhere where people see it as they come in is ideal. Placing it near the refreshments is also a good idea.
- Put up a sign guiding attendees to the table.
- Mention that your book is available at the table.
- Sit or stand near the table just before and/or during breaks so that people who come over to talk to you see your book.
- Offer additional products besides your book. You can design materials to supplement your book which are specifically geared towards seminar participants, such as literature focused on specific topics, audio and video material recording previous seminars, and audio and visual material expanding on select topics that you were unable to cover or cover completely during this seminar. You can also sell other books, literature, and non-written

materials produced by you. Related materials can be combined into packages offered at a discounted price. You may be able to make arrangements with other authors or merchants to sell their products during their seminar for a percentage of the profits.

- Include literature attendees can take home describing other products you have available, and include a copy of this literature in any handouts you distribute. (This is one method you can use to promote your book at seminars sponsored by organizations which will not allow you to sell your book directly at the seminar.)

- Bring enough products to sell to at least 10% of your audience. If your products are truly in demand by your audience, you can bring enough products for up to 40%.

- Offer discounted prices to seminar participants.

- Place a free handout at your book table near your book, and announce that this handout is available at the table.

- Have a drawing for a free copy of your book.

- Be prepared to accept checks and credit cards. Include a sign indicating what methods of payment you accept.

- Hire temporary help to help distribute your book if you expect heavy volume or if you will be distracted by other things.

- Pass around a sign-up sheet with a space for contact information so you can add your attendees to your in-house mailing list. You will get more sign-ups if you include an incentive, such as free seminar notes, a free seminar recording, or a free copy of your book.

By using these methods, your seminar can become a powerful tool for distributing your book to targeted prospects. Running seminars and answering questions from participants will also help prepare you for answering questions from the media: the final prong of your publicity campaign.

CHAPTER 19

Interviews

Answering questions from your speaking and teaching audiences will help prepare you for answering interview questions from the media, which is another cost-efficient way to promote your book. Today interviews can often be done remotely over the phone or video conference, though in some cases you may have to travel to a studio.

If you're already doing speaking or teaching, you already have most of the skills you need to promote yourself successfully through interviews. To round off your skill set, let's briefly discuss:

- How to prepare for interviews
- How to do interviews
- How to book interviews

Preparing for Interviews

Preparing for interviews is a lot like preparing for speeches or seminars. The key difference is that your control over topic selection is more limited because your host has discretion. But you can strongly influence the direction of the interview through your preparation.

Before an interview, it is a good practice to prepare a list of questions you anticipate you may be asked. You can also send a suggested question list to your interviewer to help them prepare. Try to suggest questions that point towards your book's USP. You might suggest questions about the audience your book addresses, the issues your book addresses, the benefits your book offers, or your competition.

You should also prepare a set of three index cards—one for the producer, one for the host, and one for the station's phone operator—containing the name of your book, your name, your publisher, the price, and a toll-free order number or website.

Another good practice is to offer some type of free giveaway during your interview. This gives you an opportunity to get potential customers to contact you. Your free giveaway could be your book itself, a list of tips, an informative brochure, a trivia quiz, a small gift, or some other inexpensive item which is useful, informative, or entertaining.

If you are doing an interview locally, you can boost book distribution by making agreements with local bookstores to plug them on the air if they stock a dozen copies of your book.

Doing Interviews

One of the most important things to do during an interview is relax. Before the interview, practice the same relaxation techniques suggested for speeches, using visual and auditory cues, progressive muscle relaxation, and deep breathing to relax yourself. During the interview, if you are interviewing over the phone, stand up while talking so that you can breathe more freely. If you are on TV, sit up straight, smile, and look at the interviewer rather than the camera. Observe the interviewer's body language to distract yourself from your own anxiety.

It is vital to speak clearly. Breathe slowly, talk slowly, and enunciate each word. If possible, have handy a glass of slightly warm water mixed with a dash of lemon juice to keep your throat from getting dry.

Take opportunities to plug yourself and your book. Mention your book's title and ordering information, offer your free giveaway, and comment on current news items or controversial topics.

If the interviewer asks you a question about an area you'd prefer not to get into, offer an excuse for not commenting, and change the topic to something you feel more comfortable discussing. For instance, you might say that you can't comment because you're not an expert in that area, and use that as a transition to remind them what you are an expert in.

Record your interview, or send the station a tape and ask them to record it for you, so that you can study your performance later and learn from it. You can usually also persuade the station to give you rights to the interview so that you can distribute it as a promotional piece or information product.

Booking Interviews

How do you get interviews? You can approach potential interviewers by sending them a cover letter or press release with a copy of your book. Follow up with a phone call. Your cover letter or press release should emphasize what beneficial information you have to offer the interviewer's audience, rather than emphasizing your book directly.

Who should you approach? Since there are so many radio and TV stations out there, and many of them only reach limited audiences, it is more time-efficient for you to focus on ones reaching larger audiences. However, you may choose to start with smaller audiences to give yourself an opportunity to practice doing interviews and build your confidence. You can then cite these interviews as credentials when approaching other interviewers.

Directories of media outlets which do interviews are available. There are also companies which facilitate the production and distribution of video interviews, usually for a significant fee.

Resources include:

- *Bacon's Radio/TV/Cable Directory*: http://us.cision.com/products_services/bacons_media_directories_2010.asp

- Bradley Communications' *Radio-TV Interview Report*: http://www.rtir.com/index.html

- Ericho Communications: http://www.erichopr.com

- Gordon's Radio List: http://www.radiopublicity.net

- GuestFinder.com: http://www.guestfinder.com

- Radio Publicity: http://www.radiopublicity.com

- Planned Television Arts: http://www.plannedtvarts.com/about/index.html

- Joe Sabah's *How to Get on Radio Talk Shows All Across America Without Leaving Your Home or Office*: http://www.sabahradioshows.com

- Synaptic Digital: http://www.synapticdigital.com

- *TALKERS* Magazine: http://www.talkers.com

Once you're booking regular interviews, congratulations! You are now a recognized expert! Now let's talk about how you stay recognized.

CHAPTER 20

Following Up Your Publicity Push

The strategies outlined in the previous chapters should be employed not in isolation, but as prongs of a single publicity campaign. It is important to plan your publicity push in stages so that it sustains momentum beyond your initial surge. Otherwise you risk working hard for 15 minutes of fame only to fall out of the limelight and behind your competitors again. To sustain your publicity push and maintain your expert status, you should plan a publicity timetable that regularly reinforces your audience's awareness of you:

- During the first 3 to 6 months of your publicity campaign, plan to publicize yourself to your target audience at least 4 to 6 times.

- After 6 months, continue publicizing yourself to reach your target audience at least 6 times over the next 6 months.

- After 12 months, you can reduce your publicity schedule to 4 times over the next 12 months.

- After 24 months, you can maintain your status by publicizing yourself 2 to 3 times a year.

Soon into the first months of your publicity push, your book will already be in the hands of prospects. It's time to start turning your prospects into customers.

PART V

Prospect

Your publicity campaign has succeeded in putting your book into the hands of prospective customers. How do you go about turning them into actual customers? In this section we'll cover three steps in the prospecting process:

- How to use your book to attract qualified prospects
- How to handle your initial contact with prospects who have read your book
- How to convert prospects into customers without using high-pressure sales tactics

This three-step approach will let your book make your sales for you, enabling you to convert prospects into customers without traditional sales anxiety.

CHAPTER 21

Using Your
Book to Prospect

Your book serves as a powerful prospecting tool to simplify the sales process for you. It attracts qualified prospects, enabling you to focus your sales efforts on readers who are already interested in your product or service. It allows you to pitch your sales message to different groups of qualified prospects at the same time. It enables you to motivate qualified prospects to contact you on their own initiative, taking the burden of sales anxiety off your shoulders. Let's talk about how to use your book to make the prospecting process easy for you.

The Purpose of Prospecting

The term "prospecting" calls up the image of a miner sifting through a pan of dirt looking for gold. The purpose of prospecting is to separate prospects who are potential buyers from those who aren't before you attempt any sales pitch. This saves you the time of trying to sell to someone who isn't going to buy from you no matter what you say, and it allows you to concentrate your efforts on those who are likely to buy.

Qualified vs. Non-Qualified Prospects

In sales language, a "prospect" is someone who's listening to your sales pitch, instead of walking away, slamming the door, or hanging up the phone. A "qualified prospect" is someone who wants what you're offering and is able to buy it.

There are a few major reasons why a prospect might not be qualified:

- They don't need what you're selling.
- They can't afford what you're selling.
- They don't have decision-making power within their organization to authorize a purchase.

Concentrating your sales efforts on qualified prospects is more efficient than trying to sell to non-qualified prospects. You can determine whether a prospect is qualified or not by asking pre-qualifying questions before making a sales pitch.

One advantage of your book is that you can build prequalifying information into the book. You can answer questions about who might benefit from your product or service, as well as who doesn't need it. You can also indicate prices, or at least a price range, if appropriate. By providing readers with this type of information ahead of time, you increase the odds that prospects who contact you will be qualified prospects.

Types of Qualified Prospects

Qualified prospects divide into five main groups, each requiring a different sales strategy:

- Those who need your product or service but aren't aware it exists. This group needs to be made aware of their need and the fact that there's a solution to it.

- Those who want the type of product or service you offer but are debating between you and your competition. This group needs to be convinced you can deliver more than the competition.

- Those who want what you offer but have tried your competition and are skeptical that you're any better. This group needs to be convinced you're offering something different than what they've already tried.

- Those who've already tried out several of your competitors claiming to offer something "new." This group needs to be convinced that your innovation works better than your competition's.

- Those who have grown so disillusioned with your competition that they no longer trust anyone in your industry. This group needs to be convinced that you empathize with their skepticism.

Which group predominates in your market will depend on how new your niche is and how competitive it is. If you know which group predominates in your market, you can address that group's concerns in your book. This allows your book to deliver key elements of your sales pitch for you before you ever meet your prospect.

Using Your Book to Get Qualified Prospects to Contact You

One of the most important elements of a sales pitch is a call to action. You can use your book to call prospects to act by contacting you. There are a few keys to doing this effectively.

- First, your book should end with instructions encouraging your readers to contact you. Such instructions can be direct or indirect. They can take such forms as a statement in your conclusion, a catalog, an order form, a discount offer, or a bonus offer.

- Your contact instructions must include contact information.

- The easier you can make it for readers to follow your contact instructions, the better your response will be. Consider including a reply form, such as an order form that can be torn out and mailed in.

- You can further increase your response rate by including an incentive for responding, such as a free sample, a free trial, or a free consultation.

Getting your prospect to contact you is a huge step towards converting them from a prospect into a customer. The next step is how you follow up when they contact you.

CHAPTER 22

Prospecting before Selling

When a reader of your book first contacts you, you have a prospect, but you do not yet have a customer. If you launch into a heavy-handed sales pitch immediately, you may lose a potential customer. It is usually more effective to treat your initial contact with your prospect as another stage of the qualifying process rather than as an occasion for a sales pitch. Find out what your prospect needs and help them evaluate whether what you have can meet their needs before trying to sell them something. Here are some guidelines to help you go about that.

Start by Building a Relationship

When you first meet someone, you usually start by exchanging introductions and getting to know the other person. If you have something in common, a relationship develops. If you don't, you part ways.

Traditional sales training has ignored this natural model. The traditional salesman is trained to read a script, not build a relationship. Within a few seconds of ringing your doorbell or phone, they're asking you if you're interested in buying something. If you say you're not interested, they start interrogating you and arguing with you. This displays all the finesse of a drunk who approaches a woman he doesn't know with a crude pick-up line.

It rarely works, and traditional sales tactics don't work any better. Salesmen are trained to accept the idea that dozens of rejections are normal, rather than an indicator of an inherently flawed method.

Fortunately, recent sales training has reconsidered the traditional approach and developed better methods. Building a relationship with a prospect works much better than trying to shove an artificial sales script down their throats.

How to Start Building a Relationship During Your Initial Contact

Here are some tips to help you start building a relationship with a prospect during your initial contact. These guidelines are geared towards an initial phone conversation, but they can be adapted to other media.

- Shift your focus to building a relationship with your prospect during your first contact. Shift away from worrying about getting an appointment or sale. Don't worry about achieving a predetermined outcome to the conversation. Most sales anxiety and rejection stems from trying to force an artificial outcome on a situation rather than allowing events to take their course.

- Approach the situation from the perspective of your prospect. If you were them, how would you want to be approached? What would turn you off? Think of things salesmen say and do that turn you off and resolve to avoid those things. Resolve instead to approach your prospect the way you would like to be approached. TIP: Avoid opening by asking things like "Would you be interested in. . .?" or "Do you have a few minutes?" Saying anything like that is a sure way to sound like a salesman. It projects a lack of confidence and trustworthiness. It also poses a "yes or no" question, which subconsciously encourages the prospect to say "no" to end the conversation there to get rid of you. Use open-ended questions to stimulate the conversation.

- Start the contact by exchanging introductions as you would in a normal conversation. Do not immediately start talking about your company, product, or service.

- Follow up introductions by asking if they can help you. This deliberately reverses the usual sales tactic of asking if you can help them, which sounds like sales talk and subconsciously puts them on the defensive. If you solicit help instead, most people will ask what they can help you with, which creates a positive atmosphere.

- You can then elaborate that you need help answering questions about whether they're struggling with whatever issue it is your product or service addresses. Focus on your prospect's needs. Don't launch into a speech about what you offer.

- Engage in a dialogue, not a monologue. Ask your prospect questions about their needs and answer questions they may have. Use survey questions if you find it helpful, but don't force the conversation to follow a sales script.

- Agree with objections by assuring the prospect that they're not a problem, and go on to explain why. Don't start an argument or pressure them.

- Allow the prospect to determine how the initial contact ends and whether follow-up action is appropriate. Ask them where you should go from here, and let them broach the possibility of an appointment or sale. Don't try to force a continued relationship on someone who doesn't want one. If they want to pursue further contact, they will let you know.

These guidelines will help you keep the focus of your initial contact on building a relationship focused on your prospect's needs. If you and your prospect agree on follow-up contact, you are a step closer to turning your prospect into a customer.

CHAPTER 23

Selling by Listening

If your prospect expresses interest in follow-up contact, you have an opportunity to close a sale. Traditional sales training seeks to achieve this by following a sales script. There is a more effective way to close sales, and it is also simpler: instead of talking, listen.

Listen to Their Needs

Asking about your prospect's needs during your initial contact sets the tone for your relationship. Asking follow-up questions gives you an opportunity to further qualify them and evaluate whether your product or service might help them. You can ask questions about:

- The experiences that prompted them to contact you
- How they got started in their business or the situation that they came to you about
- The issues they face
- The concerns they have
- Their goals
- Their priorities
- Their previous experience with other products or services

- How they decided to buy previous products or services
- How they will decide to buy future products or services
- Whether they have any questions they'd like to ask you

In some cases you may find it useful to create a form to standardize questions for new prospects and record answers.

As you listen to your prospect's answers to your questions, evaluate whether what they need matches what your product or service offers.

Echo Their Needs in Your Offer

If it sounds like your product or service can help your prospect, offer to help them. Your offer will get the warmest reception if you express it in language that echoes the needs the prospect expressed to you. Here are some ways to put your offer into language that will address your prospect's needs:

1. Listen carefully to identify what is most important to your prospect. Listen for keywords the prospect has emphasized. Listen to the order of priority they have ranked those keywords in.

2. Ask questions that echo back the prospect's priorities to make sure you have understood them correctly. Be sure to use the exact words the prospect has emphasized in the exact order that is important to them. Do not substitute your own interpretations or priorities for theirs. If you are not sure what they mean by a certain word or phrase, ask follow-up questions until you are clear on what it ultimately means to them. If you are not sure which priority ranks higher for them, try changing the order to see how they react. Their reaction will tell you if you have understood their priorities correctly.

3. After you are sure you understand the prospect's priorities correctly, ask them what would be the next step if they found a solution that met those priorities. If they do not indicate the next step is a purchase, you are missing some information they need to make a buying decision and should review the previous steps.

4. Present your product or service as a solution to your prospect's needs, using the same language the prospect used to describe those needs to you, and ask what the next step should be.

If you follow this strategy correctly, you will not need to memorize a script to close the sale. If you make the effort to listen to what your prospect needs and offer what they want, they will ask you how much it costs without you bringing it up.

PART VI

Service=Sales

If you approach making a sale as the ultimate goal of your relationship with your customer, chances are it will be your last sale to them. Making a sale is only the beginning of your relationship with your customer. You have offered to serve their needs. Delivering that service is the culmination of the sales process and the start of your ongoing relationship with your customer.

So the next step of promoting your book is following through on your book's offer with customer service. This includes:

- Delivering what you promised your customer and overdelivering to exceed their expectations
- Appreciating the lifetime value of your customers beyond your initial sales to them
- Soliciting customer feedback in order to make your future products and services meet their needs even better

Our remaining discussion will focus on these topics.

CHAPTER 24

Selling
by Service

Customer service is following through on the offer you promised in your book and your follow-up contact with your customer. Delivering what you promised is the minimum requirement to fulfill your promise. Overdelivering more than you promised is the key to keeping your customer enthusiastic about your service. Measuring how well you're delivering gives you objective feedback you can use to evaluate your performance and improve it.

Delivering

Delivering what you promised brings your USP to life by giving your customer what you offered them. It also goes beyond your USP to include other elements of customer service not necessarily emphasized in your USP but equally important to your customer. You can evaluate your delivery by breaking it down into questions about specific categories, such as:

- Did I maintain a positive relationship with my customer throughout my service to them?
- Did I solve the problem my customer came to me for help with?
- Did I bring my customer the benefits I promised?

- Did I deliver my services to my customer on time?
- Did I deliver my services to my customer at the price I promised?
- Did I include any bonuses I promised?
- Did I follow through on any guarantees?
- Did I leave my customer more satisfied than previous vendors they have dealt with?
- Did I say thank you?

Asking these kinds of questions can help you focus on specific aspects of your delivery for evaluation and improvement.

Overdelivering

Overdelivery means delivering more than you promised. It is what separates a satisfied customer from an enthusiastic customer eager for more interaction with you. You can evaluate overdelivery by extrapolating from the same types of questions you used to evaluate your delivery:

- Did I make my customer feel special?
- Did I help them solve even more problems than they came to me about?
- Did I deliver even more benefits than I promised?
- Did I deliver service even faster than expected?
- Did I save my customer even more money than they were expecting?
- Did I surprise my customer with any additional bonuses?
- Did I go out of my way to make sure my customer was compensated for any dissatisfaction?
- Did I encourage my customer to compare me to the competition and hold me to a superior standard?

- Did I say thank you in more than just words by giving my customer something as an expression of appreciation?

Your performance in these areas is what will keep your customers coming back to you.

Measuring Your Performance

How do you measure how well you're delivering and overdelivering to your customers? You can perform your own self-evaluation, which is a start. But it's more objective and valuable to solicit your customer's feedback. You can do this by:

- Creating a follow-up mechanism to collect customer feedback, such as a questionnaire
- Offering an incentive for customers to participate in your feedback program, such as a bonus
- Publicizing the results of your customer feedback

Measuring your performance will help you turn customers into repeat customers, which is a key to continued business growth and our next subject.

CHAPTER 25

Creating
Lifetime Customers

Superior customer service maximizes your odds of turning your customers into repeat customers, which can multiply your profits enormously. Repeat customers are more likely than any other target market to buy products and services from you. Repeat customers are also likely to make referrals, your best source of new prospects.

Appreciating Lifetime Value over Single Sales

The traditional sales approach of measuring success by single sales is short-sighted. The value of a single sale pales in comparison to the lifetime value of a satisfied customer. Unlike a new prospect, a satisfied customer:

- Already has a relationship with you
- Is already prequalified
- Is already sold on your line of products or services
- Is already sold on your credibility
- Already has a billing account with you

For these reasons, it is far more efficient to focus your marketing efforts on existing customers than on new prospects. This is why direct mail marketers prize in-house mailing lists above all other mailing lists.

Sales Multipliers: Bundling, Cross-Sells, Upsells, and Downsells

A customer is most likely to buy from you while they are buying something else from you. A customer making a purchase is in a buying mood. Because of this, the most effective way to market to existing customers is to offer other items while they are making a purchase.

The practice of offering several items as a package is known as "bundling." The classic example is McDonald's famous question, "Would you like some fries with that?"

Bundling overlaps with three related sales tactics that have proven effective for multiplying sales:

- Cross-sells: A cross-sell offers an item complementing the customer's current purchase. An example is to offer a customer purchasing an electronic item a discount on batteries.

- Upsells: An upsell offers to upgrade the customer's purchase to a higher-priced item or package, often discounted from its regular price as an incentive. An example is to offer a customer purchasing software a special price on a deluxe edition of the same software.

- Downsells: A downsell makes a lower-priced offer to someone who has rejected a higher price for the same item or a similar item. An example is to offer a customer who has rejected a deluxe software package a lower-priced version of the same software with fewer features.

These tactics may also be sequenced over time rather than deployed at the moment of purchase. When selling information products, an effective sequenced upselling strategy is to offer higher-priced services, such as seminars and coaching, to customers who have previously purchased lower-priced information products.

Additional items included in bundled packages, cross-sells, upsells, and downsells can be your own products or services, or products and services of your business allies.

To illustrate how some of these tactics might be used with a book, let's imagine a company that sells survival gear. The company publishes a book about strategies for surviving natural disasters. The book leads the reader to an e-commerce website, where they decide to purchase some freeze-dried food. Upon purchasing the food, the checkout page offers them an upsell discount on a windpower generator. You can imagine numerous similar examples for different industries.

Joint Venture Cross-Promotions

A business ally who works with you on a promotion is known as a *joint venture partner* (*JV partner*). You can use joint-venture cross-promotions when applying the strategies of bundling, cross-selling, upselling, and downselling. You can also do joint venture cross-promotions independent of these strategies.

There are two major types of joint venture cross-promotions:

- Promotions where your joint venture partners promote you to their customers in return for a commission or other considerations
- Promotions where you promote your joint venture partners to your customers in return for a commission or other considerations

Earning commissions by promoting your joint venture partners to your customers is another way to increase the lifetime value of your customers. When promoting joint-venture partners, go out of your way to screen your partners and their products and services and make sure they are in your customers' best interests. Promoting a bad product or service to your customers will backfire badly.

Referrals

When measuring your customer's lifetime value, you should appreciate not only the purchases that customer makes, but also the referrals they generate. Referrals from satisfied customers are your best source of new prospects. Referrals are the most effective form of publicity because:

- Your customers already know the needs of prospects they refer you to, so the prospects are qualified.
- Your customers are already known to your prospects, increasing your credibility.
- Your customers' use of your product or service provides a live demonstration.
- Your customers' enthusiasm for your product or service provides a spontaneous testimonial.
- Your customers' referrals are free publicity.

Because referrals are so powerful, you should make a special effort to cultivate them. You can do this by applying the strategies suggested when we were discussing word-of-mouth promotion, in Chapter 13, "Word-of-Mouth Publicity: Referrals and Endorsements." In that context we were primarily concerned with cultivating referrals for your book. But in a broader context, you should cultivate referrals for all aspects of your business.

One way we suggested to cultivate referrals was to ask your customers to test market new products and services. This topic brings us full circle back to market research, where we started our book publicity strategy and where we will end.

CHAPTER 26

Investing in Research and Development

We started our book publicity strategy with market research, and we now return full circle to our starting point. Sales success provides you with fuel for more market research to keep your sales cycle moving forward. As you make sales, you earn profits that you can invest in market research and research and development. You gain customer feedback that you can use to guide your research and development. And you gain a test market that can help you refine products and services you're getting ready to launch.

Investing Your Profits

One of the best ways to capitalize on sales success is to invest a percentage of your profits in market research and research and development of new products and services. This grows your business in two ways:

- Market research tells you what needs are in demand.
- Research and development provides you with new products and services to meet those needs.

By investing your profits in these areas, your initial business success in one market becomes a catapult propelling you to success in multiple markets. You also ensure that you stay on the cutting edge of the market instead of falling behind your competitors.

Listening to Customer Feedback

As you begin a new phase of market research, the best research resource available is your existing customers. You can tap into this resource by:

- Asking your customers what they liked and disliked about your product or service
- Asking what they'd like to see in the future
- Rewarding them for taking the time to answer your questions

In this way your existing customers can provide you with a cost-efficient way to conduct high-quality market research on a highly-targeted test group.

Test-Launching New Products and Services

Your existing customers can also help you test-market new products and services you're getting ready to launch. You can ask customers to help you test out new products and services in return for a free version, a bonus, or a discount. This provides you and your customers several advantages:

- It makes your customers feel special and builds your relationship with them.
- It allows your customers to try out your new product or service without the pressure of a buying decision.
- It provides you with feedback you can use to fix problems and improve your launch before offering it to a larger audience.
- It generates pre-publicity for your new launch.

Your Book as a Marketing Investment

The above suggestions apply to your business in general. You can also apply them specifically to your book in several ways:

- Invest a percentage of profits from your book in market research and research and development.

- Include a reader feedback response mechanism in your book to solicit market research information. The mechanism can take such forms as a mail-in form or a link to an online survey. You will get the best response if you include an incentive.

- Offer readers of your book a preview of your new product or service. This offer can be tied into your reader feedback response mechanism. For instance, you can extend all readers who participate in a feedback survey an offer of a free test drive of an upcoming launch.

- Use reader feedback as material for a new book.

By applying these suggestions, your book becomes not only a publicity tool promoting your current business, but an investment promoting your future business growth.

PART VII

Putting It into Practice

We've now covered all the steps in the REAPS book publicity strategy:

Research your market

Express your message

Announce your book to the world

Prospect for customers

Service=Sales

As with anything, knowing the theory is only half the battle. Putting it into practice is the greater challenge. To help you put this book's suggestions into practice, we will round up with a discussion of mistakes to avoid, before concluding with advice on how to leverage your book into business success.

CHAPTER 27

25 Common Mistakes to Avoid

Removing barriers to a goal is often the quickest way to achieve the goal. Because of this, it's always good to be aware of mistakes to avoid. Mistakes can be made in any of the numerous areas we have discussed. Here we're just going to list 25 common ones to avoid when conducting your book publicity campaign:

Marketing Mistakes

1. Failing to define your audience

A perfectly-written commercial for shampoo will have no effect on a bald man.

2. Failing to research your competition

You cannot offer something different than your competition if you don't know what they're offering.

3. Failing to address a need

If you don't tell your audience what your book can help them with, how will they know?

4. Failing to emphasize benefits

Your audience doesn't want to know what your product or service is; they want to know how it can help them.

5. Failing to define your USP

Why should your audience read your book instead of doing something else?

Writing Mistakes

6. Picking an unmarketable topic

Is your topic something you want to talk about instead of something your audience wants to hear about?

7. Picking a bad title

Does your title tell your audience what your book is about or does it just sound pretty?

8. Picking bad chapter titles and subheadings

Could a reader follow your train of thought just by reading your table of contents?

9. Stylistic problems

If a sixth grader would have trouble understanding your book, it's too hard to read. If your book looks like it was written by a sixth grader, you need an editor.

10. Poor cover design

Showcasing your USP through your title should take precedence over graphics, but an eye-catching design is also a plus.

Promotional Mistakes

11. Failing to take responsibility for promotion because you're relying on your publisher

Don't assume that just because your book is published it's going to sell itself.

12. Paying for advertising instead of publicity

The traditional marketing advice to throw money at advertising is the wrong way to sell a book.

13. Failing to emphasize your USP in your promotions

The purpose of your book and your book promotions is to promote your USP, so don't forget to mention it.

14. Lack of response mechanism

Make sure your audience knows how to contact you.

15. Failure to maintain your status

After you've worked so hard to gain publicity, don't rest on your laurels and let your competition creep up on you.

Prospecting Mistakes

16. Focusing on trying to get an appointment or sale instead of serving your prospect's needs

Put your focus on your prospect and it will distract you from your sales anxiety.

17. Skipping to sales without qualifying your prospect

Don't waste your prospect's time or your own trying to sell something to someone who doesn't want it or can't afford it.

18. Reading from a sales script instead of listening

Talk with your prospect, not at them.

19. Failing to identify your prospect's priorities

Base your conversation on what's important to your prospect.

20. Trying to force a close

Match your offer to your prospect's needs and you won't need to worry about closing.

Sales and Service Mistakes

21. Failing to track customer service performance

Don't guess how you're doing; ask your customers.

22. Focusing on single sales instead of customer lifetime value

Don't miss the forest for the trees.

23. Failing to ask customers for referrals

Asking for referrals will multiply your chances of getting them.

24. Failing to solicit customer feedback

Don't overlook your best source of market research.

25. Failing to invest in research and development

Invest your money to make it grow.

There are many other possible mistakes you can make, and many you probably will make. We make them ourselves all the time, and we've probably made a few in this book. No one is perfect. But if you at least know to avoid these, and you can avoid a few of them, you've got a big head start over someone who doesn't even know what to look out for.

Building on Your Book

Throughout this book, we've emphasized how publicizing your book can promote your business. Along the way, we've drawn attention to ways book publicity can expand your business in new directions, including:

- Future books and articles
- Digital information products
- Public speaking events
- Private teaching programs and consultations
- Joint venture alliances

Each of these areas in itself is potentially profitable. And each of these areas can mutually stimulate the others, creating a profit multiplier effect. By leveraging your book into these opportunities, you can expand your business far beyond your current line of products or services to multiply your profits exponentially.

We close, then, by encouraging you to think of your book not just as a publicity tool, but as the foundation of your own financial empire. This is the concealed power of the pen that is mightier than the sword. This is the power of the press unleashed. This is the full power of publishing for publicity.

For More Information

If you have questions about any of the topics covered in this book, or if you are seeking professional assistance in writing, publishing, or promoting your book, please do not hesitate to contact us. We are happy to answer your questions, and we provide a full range of writing-related services, including:

- Market research
- Library research
- Online research
- Ghostwriting
- Copywriting
- Editing
- Proofreading
- Book interior design
- Cover design
- Traditional marketing consultation, including development of Unique Sales Propositions, direct marketing, and joint venture strategies
- Internet marketing consultation, including keyword research and search engine optimization
- Traditional publicity consultation, including press kit creation and rehearsing and arranging media appearances
- Online publicity consultation, including video marketing and social media marketing
- Mobile phone marketing

We offer a free initial consultation for qualified applicants. Please let us know how we can help you get your book published and publicized.

Roy Rasmussen

Marian Hartsough

Publishing Alternatives
1285 Stratford Avenue, Suite G262
Dixon, CA 95620
1-866-221-8408
http://publishingforpublicity.com

About the Authors

ROY RASMUSSEN is a freelance writing consultant who specializes in showcasing his clients' unique marketing strengths. He draws from his marketing training, technical writing background, and copywriting experience to create readable information products promoting his clients' expertise. Over the past 20 years his clients have included banks, tax advisors, accountants, insurance companies, real estate agents, power companies, sports injury therapists, herbalists, political organizations, comic book historians, software designers, children's books authors, graphic designers, and publicists. He is experienced in editing and proofreading and is trained in illustration, animation, and video production. He holds degrees in philosophy, theology, and history and has won an award for his writing on the philosophical implications of quantum physics. His ghostwriting on herbalism has been used to teach writing courses by Emmy-winning scriptwriter Patrick Nolan, cowriter of *Miami Vice* executive producer Michael Mann.

MARIAN HARTSOUGH is a publishing consultant who provides independent authors with editorial, book design, and publicity support comparable to major publishers, but distinguished by custom-designed individual attention and customer service. Trained at Harper & Row, over the past 30 years she has provided professional editing and book design services for clients such as Random House, Prima Publishing, McGraw-Hill, Thomson Learning, Course Technology, Michigan University Press, and Bank of America. She supervises a full book production team of writers, editors, illustrators, cover designers, proofreaders, and publicists. She and her team have produced more than 500 books. She holds a degree in anthropology from the University of California, Berkeley. She has extensive training in traditional publicity and Internet marketing and is currently supervising production of a book on TV publicity. Marian lives in Northern California on a farm full of horses, llamas, peacocks, and other assorted critters.